How to Lease Space in Shopping Centers

How to Lease Space in Shopping Centers

◆

A Guide for Small Business Owners

Barry Fleisher

iUniverse, Inc.
New York Lincoln Shanghai

How to Lease Space in Shopping Centers
A Guide for Small Business Owners

iUniverse, Inc.

For information address:
iUniverse, Inc.
2021 Pine Lake Road, Suite 100
Lincoln, NE 68512
www.iuniverse.com

ISBN: 0-595-28263-6

Printed in the United States of America

Contents

About the Book

The purpose of *How to Lease Space in Shopping Centers: A Guide for Small Business Owners* is to assist the owners of small retail and service business in leasing spaces in shopping centers, from large regional shopping malls to small strip centers.

Small owners of local businesses who rent space in shopping centers are at a disadvantage. Most of the shopping center spaces are leased to national chain stores, which have a professional and experienced real estate staff to assist in finding a good location and negotiating a lease with some terms favorable to the tenant. A local business owner usually chooses a shopping center close to home and tries to negotiate a lease without any professional assistance. In most cases, small business owners accept the terms of the standard lease offered by the landlord and seldom attempt to negotiate any changes to the terms or conditions of the lease.

Shopping Centers are developed and leased for the benefit of the landlord, or owner of the shopping center. The leases in the center are drafted to favor the landlord. It is not unusual to have a lease clause in a pre-printed lease that has been routinely deleted or altered by every national tenant. But almost every local tenant who signs the lease accepts the clause without questioning it.

A review of a file drawer full of leases in a shopping center management office will easily show which lease belongs to a local tenant and which leases belong to national tenants: the pages of the local tenant's lease are clean. There are no changes, deletions, or additions to the pre-written lease. Some national tenants' leases have changes on nearly every page, all designed to make sure the tenant gets a favorable deal.

In most cases, the local tenant mistakenly assumes that all the tenants in the shopping center are under the same terms and conditions, and that all tenants are paying about the same rent and other additional rent expenses. The reality is that the local tenants often pay the highest possible rate for CAM fees and other fees due to the wording of the provisions in the leases. The irony, of course, is that you are probably the one who can least afford to pay the highest fees.

Can you get the same deal as a national chain store? Probably not, because the national chain store will take more space, sell more products, pay more rent, and offer a better credit rating than most local tenants. But you can be successful in getting many favorable changes to a lease deal. You might not get everything, but you can get some changes that will help reduce costs, and offer some protection against future consequences.

You have many different options available when considering a lease in a shopping center, and this book discusses all of them: carts, kiosk, in-line spaces, temporary tenant arrangements, incubator deals, percentage-only rent, free rent, gross rent, and improvements to the space. Many start-up business owners choose to follow a non-traditional plan for leasing a shopping center space, perhaps by starting small with a temporary lease at a lower rent. To be able to negotiate a deal that will help you get started you must understand how the shopping center leasing game works and what options might be available. The shopping center leasing agent won't offer many creative deals.

The book is valuable for existing tenants whose leases are coming up for renewal and renegotiation. Any small business with a good track record is in a much stronger position to negotiate more favorable terms into the lease at renewal time.

The shopping center business is increasingly risky for small business owners. Anchor stores that drive traffic to shopping centers have closed. Department store chains have merged and consolidated. A shopping center that has been a great location for years can suddenly be a death trap. Without negotiating some protection into the lease ahead of time, these events and circumstances can wipe out you out. This book tells how to get sales kick-outs, co-occupancy clauses and other agreements into the lease as protection against future problems.

A word about legal advice: This book is not a replacement for good legal advice when it comes to signing a lease or any kind of legal agreement. This book is intended to advise how to negotiate favorable *business terms* to a lease—it does not address the many *legal terms* that are an important part of any contract. It is always wise to have an attorney review your lease, after you have negotiated the best possible business terms for the deal. It is always smart to find an attorney who is experienced with shopping centers and leases.

Shopping centers are great locations for small businesses, and offer the best locations for a profitable and successful business. You can improve the chances for your success by negotiating a good shopping center deal ahead of time. Good luck and best wishes for future success!

1

TYPES OF SHOPPING CENTERS

◆

Select the right type of shopping center for your business location

There are two categories of shopping centers—enclosed malls and open strip centers. This chapter will describe each type of shopping center so you can choose the best location for your business.

Owners of shopping centers are usually real estate development companies who built the center, or investment companies who bought the shopping center from the development company. The commercial spaces in the shopping center are usually leased to tenants, although sometimes a large store will own its own real estate under an agreement with the rest of the shopping center.

The owner of a shopping center in a lease is referred to as the *Landlord*, and the entity that leases the space from the landlord is called the *Tenant*. Sometimes the owner will be referred to as the *Developer*, especially if the owner built the shopping center.

Shopping centers house stores referred to as *anchors* or *majors*, which are the larger stores that draw traffic to the center. Some smaller centers may be *unanchored*, while some centers may have *restaurant and entertainment anchors*. The anchor store in a strip center may be a grocery store, a discount store, or a drug store. The anchor stores in enclosed malls are typically department stores.

The rest of the commercial space in the shopping center is leased to retail, service and other commercial businesses. Many of the tenants are national chain store companies. Leasing space is preferable for most businesses because they don't tie up their capital in real estate, and they are favorably located with a mass of other retail stores.

The owners of shopping centers prefer to lease space to larger, national companies because the risk of business failure is less than with a one-store owner. It is also easier for the shopping center owner to get financing with strong, national, credit tenants, than with a large percentage of local, independent tenants. Typically, the national chain tenants draw more customers, produce more sales, and pay more rent than your store.

On the other hand, small local businesses provide a local flavor and some spice to the sometimes too-ordinary mix of merchandise in the shopping center, and the owners of shopping centers need to have that variety to draw customer interest and traffic. Franchise operations are also popular with shopping center owners. The franchise business provides a local owner with the benefits of national brand recognition, product quality and retail support. In a franchise business, the tenant is usually the local owner, although sometimes the franchising company will also sign the lease.

The number of small, local businesses and franchises in a shopping center varies depending on the size of the center and its location. Although a majority of the space in some centers may be leased to national chain stores, almost all shopping centers have space available for local tenants. The smaller centers, such as neighborhood centers and community centers, have a higher percentage of local tenants and are easier to get into. Regional and super regional centers, which have a higher percentage of national retailers, are often harder for you to enter. However, even the larger centers have space available for good local tenants and the high traffic of these centers provide great locations for your business.

The International Council of Shopping Centers defines two basic configurations and several shopping center types[1]:

---

1.   International Council of Shopping Centers, "ICSC Shopping Center Definitions", copyright 1999.

TWO BASIC CONFIGURATIONS

Mall: Malls typically are enclosed, with a climate-controlled walkway between two facing strips of stores. The term "Mall" represents the most common design for regional and super regional centers and has become an informal term for these types of centers.

Strip Center: A strip center is an attached row of stores or service outlets managed as a coherent retail entity, with on-site parking usually located in front of the stores. Open canopies may connect the storefronts, but a strip center does not have enclosed walkways linking the stores. A strip center may be configured in a straight line, or have an "L" or "U" shape.

TYPES OF MALLS AND STRIP CENTERS

Neighborhood Center: This center is designed to provide convenience for the day-to-day needs of consumers in the immediate neighborhood. A supermarket anchors about half of these centers, while about a third have a drugstore anchor. The types of stores typically found in Neighborhood Centers are those offering health-related products, sundries, snacks, and personal services.

Community Center: A community center typically offers a wider range of apparel and other soft goods than the neighborhood center. Common anchors include supermarkets, super drugstores, and discount department stores. Community center tenants include off-price retailers selling apparel, home improvement/home furnishings, toys, electronics, and sporting goods. Community centers encompass the widest range of formats, such as "Discount Centers" or "Off-Price Centers".

Regional Center: This center provides general merchandise, including a large percentage of apparel, and services in full depth and variety. The main attractions are the anchors: traditional, mass merchant, discount department stores, or fashion specialty stores. A typical regional center is usually an enclosed shopping mall with an inward orientation of the stores connected by a common walkway. Parking surrounds the outside perimeter.

Super Regional Center: This center is similar to a regional center, but is larger and has more anchors, a deeper selection of merchandise, and draws from a larger population base. The typical configuration is an enclosed mall, frequently with multiple levels.

Fashion/Specialty Center: This center is composed mainly of upscale apparel shops, boutiques, and craft shops. Stores carry fashions and unique merchandise of high quality and price. These centers are not always anchored, although sometimes restaurants and entertainment can provide the draw of anchors. The physical design of the center is very sophisticated, emphasizing a rich décor and high quality landscaping. These centers are usually found in high-income areas.

Power Center: Several large anchors dominate this center, including discount department stores, off-price stores, warehouse clubs, and "category killers", which are stores that offer a large selection in a particular merchandise category at low prices. The center typically consists of several freestanding and unconnected anchors and only a minimum of small specialty tenants.

Theme/Festival Center: These centers typically employ a unifying theme that is carried out by the individual shops in their architectural design and in their merchandise. Restaurants and entertainment facilities anchor this type of center, which appeals to tourists. Sometimes these centers are adapted from older historic buildings, and can be part of mixed-use projects.

Outlet Center: These centers are usually located in rural or tourist locations, and consist of mostly manufacturer's outlet stores selling their own brands at a discount. These centers are typically not anchored. Some are strip centers, some are enclosed malls, and others are arranged in a 'village' cluster.

Lifestyle Center: A lifestyle center is a new concept that has only recently been defined by the International Council of Shopping Centers (ICSC)[2]. This center caters to the retail needs and "lifestyle" pursuits of consumers in its trading area. Most often, they are located near affluent residential neighborhoods and have an upscale orientation. They have an open-air configuration and include upscale national chain specialty shops, restaurants and entertainment. The lifestyle center usually includes amenities such as fountains and street furniture, often reflecting a "Main Street" type of ambience.

---

2.   ICSC Research Quarterly, V. 8, No. 4—Winter 2001–02, "Lifestyle Centers—A Defining Moment".

2

HOW SHOPPING CENTERS ARE OPERATED

✦

Knowing who the players are can improve your chances of success

OWNERS

Most of the larger shopping centers today are owned or managed by a large national company. Life insurance companies, pension funds and other investment companies own many shopping centers. Ownership of many shopping malls is through a Real Estate Investment Trust (REIT), where shares are traded on the public stock exchanges, and the management company is responsible to stockholders. Several partners may own larger centers under a General Partnership or a Limited Partnership. The largest shopping mall company in the country today owns and manages more than 150 shopping malls.

Small shopping centers, such as neighborhood centers and some community centers, may be locally owned and operated.

MANAGEMENT COMPANIES

Usually, there is a separate company or entity that manages the shopping center for the owner. Rarely does the owner of a shopping center manage the project itself. Sometimes, the owner has a subsidiary management company to manage its assets, and sometimes a separately owned company manages the asset for a fee. There are several national real estate companies that manage shopping centers for passive investor-owners.

Smaller neighborhood and community centers are more apt to be managed by a local or regional real estate company. The owner's company may operate them, or the owner may hire a separate management company and pay a fee for the management responsibilities.

Larger projects, including enclosed malls, always have an on-site management office. In some cases, there is a local leasing representative, but in many cases, the leasing is handled out of the company's home office or a regional office. Some management companies have their on-site property managers handle local leasing, while other companies have their leasing agents handle both local leasing and national leasing.

Small centers, however, may not have an on-site management office. Many times, they are managed from a central office, and the property manager and leasing agent just visit the shopping center as needed.

ON-SITE MANAGEMENT

The on-site property management office may be staffed with the following positions:

- General Manager
- Operations Manager or Assistant Manager, or both
- Marketing Director, and Assistant Marketing Director
- Leasing Agent (sometimes)
- Specialty Leasing Agent (in larger centers with a specialty leasing program)
- Administrative Assistants
- Accountants or Bookkeepers
- Maintenance Staff
- Security Staff
- Customer Service Representatives

You should talk to the General Manager and the Marketing Director, as well as the leasing agent. When dealing with an out-of-town leasing agent, you would be well advised to get to know the on-site staff. They will be dealing with problems and issues on a day-to-day basis. After the deal is made, the leasing agent may not be around.

The on-site management is responsible for operating the shopping center—keeping the common areas safe and clean, maintaining and repairing building systems and equipment, handling new construction, collecting rent, enforcing lease rules and regulations, and marketing and promoting the shopping center.

LEASING AGENTS

Every shopping center management company has leasing agents whose job is to find tenants and lease the space. In regional shopping malls operated by large companies, the leasing agent may be responsible for more than one shopping center in different cities. These agents work for the shopping center company.

Some shopping center owners may hire a local commercial real estate brokerage company to lease the space in the center. These agents are independent, working for a commission on each lease, and may represent several different shopping centers in a local area.

In larger malls, there are *specialty-leasing agents*, who lease space to temporary tenants for seasonal or short-term uses. Some shopping center managers are actively involved in leasing space to both permanent and temporary tenants. It depends on the company—some companies want their managers involved in leasing and some don't.

TENANT LEASING REPRESENTATIVES

National chain store companies employ their own leasing agents to search out good space and negotiate leases in new locations. The leasing reps know the major shopping center owners, managers, and leasing agents.

There is no one in a shopping center management team that is assigned to help or assist tenants with leasing space. The marketing director often assists tenants with retail displays and promotional opportunities, but in most cases the marketing director is not involved with leasing.

ICSC

There is a shopping center industry association, the International Council of Shopping Centers (ICSC), with chapters in the U.S., Canada and many foreign countries. ICSC sponsors local and national conferences every year where attendees can meet to negotiate new leases, and attend sessions on the shopping center industry trends and issues. Almost all shopping center managers and companies are members of ICSC.

Many shopping center leases between shopping center representatives and tenant real estate representatives are negotiated at the annual ICSC leasing convention held each May in Las Vegas, Nevada. There are also several smaller, regional leasing conventions held around the country throughout the year.

3

FINDING THE RIGHT LOCATION

✦

The two most important criteria are location and location

The two most important elements to consider in choosing a space for a retail business are location and location, meaning, the location of the shopping center within a trade area, and the location of the space within the shopping center. Choose the better of those two locations, but explore all of the choices available in your market.

You have a wide variety of choices available to choose a location for your small business: a freestanding building, a warehouse location, a downtown building, a neighborhood shopping center, a strip shopping center, or an enclosed shopping mall. Every location has its advantages and disadvantages, and the choice of where to locate a business is crucial to success.

Don't make the mistake of deciding where to locate a business solely on the basis of cost or convenience to the business owner. This is not a good way to decide on a location. Rent should not be the main consideration. A rent location is cheap because no one else wants it. Only a strong, well-established destination business can survive in a bad location. If you are trying to get a business established you are better off going where the traffic is, and that usually means paying higher rent. However, the term "high rent" is relative. Would you rather own a business doing $500,000 and paying $50,000 a year rent, or a business doing $250,000 and paying $12,000 a year rent?

COMPARING SHOPPING CENTERS IN AN AREA

There are many different ways to compare different shopping centers. When choosing a shopping center location for your business, consider the following criteria:

Demographics: Each shopping center draws from a distinct area. A small neighborhood center might draw from a 1-mile or 3-mile radius. A regional shopping mall might draw from a 30-mile radius. You can easily obtain demographic information on any location that you are considering. Most shopping center leasing agents have demographic information on their trade area, but if not, there are companies available that specialize in producing quick demographic reports.

If you are looking at two or three alternate locations, obtain a recent demographic report on each location's trade area, and select the one that offers your business the best customer base. Some things to compare on a demographic report:

Population living in the trade area. Generally the denser the population, the more traffic your location will enjoy. Most chain retail stores require a minimum population within a certain radius before they will consider opening a store in any location.

Average household income in the trade area. Higher incomes mean more disposable income.

Family size could be important, along with the average ages of the population.

Employment information might be useful for some types of businesses. So could the average education of the population.

The national chain stores know what demographic information will work for their business. Over the years, they study which of their stores are the most profitable, and which stores have been least profitable. Then, when they look for a new location for a new store, they know exactly what population density, household income, etc. they are looking for.

If you have only one or a few locations you don't have that proven experience to rely upon. Instead, find a successful business similar to the type of business you want to operate, and obtain demographic information on that business's location. Then, shop for locations for your business, and compare the demographic information on each possible site until you find the one that matches most closely with the proven successful business.

Exhibit 3-A for shows a sample of a demographic report for a 1-3-5 mile radius around a shopping center location.

SAMPLE DEMOGRAPHIC REPORT

DESCRIPTION	1.00 MILE RADIUS	3.00 MILE RADIUS	4.00 MILE RADIUS
POPULATION			
2004 PROJECTION	10,340	50,952	171,370
1999 ESTIMATE	9,893	48,581	162,385
1990 CENSUS	9,387	45,421	149,584
1980 CENSUS	9,506	42,859	136,968
GROWTH 1980–1990	-1.25%	5.98%	9.21%
HOUSEHOLDS			
2004 PROJECTION	3,381	17,024	58,373
1999 ESTIMATE	3,192	16,003	54,547
1990 CENSUS	2,948	14,495	48,721
1980 CENSUS	2,849	13,351	44,000
GROWTH 1980–1990	3.47%	8.57%	10.73%
1999 ESTIMATED POPULATION BY RACE	9,893	48,581	162,385
WHITE	25.20%	37.56%	44.55%
BLACK	68.73%	51.14%	41.00%
ASIAN & PACIFIC ISLANDER	0.62%	1.45%	1.66%
OTHER RACES	5.45%	9.85%	12.79%
1999 ESTIMATED POPULATION	9,893	48,581	162,385
HISPANIC ORIGIN	8.77%	15.96%	21.21%
OCCUPIED UNITS	2,948	14,495	48,721
OWNER OCCUPIED	84.05%	70.99%	66.84%
RENTER OCCUPIED	15.95%	29.01%	33.16%
1990 AVERAGE PERSONS PER HH	3.17	3.04	3.01
1999 EST. HOUSEHOLDS BY INCOME	3,192	16,003	54,547
$150,000 OR MORE	0.40%	1.38%	2.11%
$100,000 TO $149,999	4.62%	3.49%	5.06%
$75,000 TO $99,999	12.66%	7.98%	8.93%
$50,000 TO $74,999	24.41%	20.22%	18.93%
$35,000 TO $49,999	18.99%	16.94%	16.40%
$25,000 TO $34,999	14.29%	16.43%	14.11%
$15,000 TO $24,999	12.22%	15.61%	14.88%
$5,000 TO $14,999	8.85%	12.92%	13.90%
UNDER $5,000	3.56%	5.03%	5.68%

DESCRIPTION	1.00 MILE RADIUS	3.00 MILE RADIUS	4.00 MILE RADIUS
1999 EST. AVE. HOUSEHOLD INCOME	$49,577	$44,776	$47,537
1999 EST. MEDIAN HH INCOME	$43,748	$35,014	$36,304
1999 EST. PER CAPITA INCOME	$16,102	$15,039	$16,178
1999 ESTIMATED POPULATION BY SEX	9,893	48,581	162,385
MALE	48.70%	49.17%	48.80%
FEMALE	51.30%	50.83%	51.20%
MARITAL STATUS	6,969	33,724	110,023
SINGLE MALE	14.21%	14.53%	14.49%
SINGLE FEMALE	11.09%	11.70%	11.91%
MARRIED	55.34%	51.61%	51.80%
PREVIOUSLY MARRIED MALE	6.43%	7.90%	7.21%
PREVIOUSLY MARRIED FEMALE	12.93%	14.26%	14.58%
HOUSEHOLDS WITH CHILDREN	1,545	7,186	23,299
MARRIED COUPLE FAMILY	70.63%	64.00%	64.94%
OTHER FAMILY—MALE HEAD	6.71%	6.20%	5.67%
OTHER FAMILY—FEMALE HEAD	22.02%	28.81%	28.52%
NON FAMILY	0.64%	0.99%	0.88%
1999 EST. POPULATION BY AGE	9,893	48,581	162,385
UNDER 5 YEARS	7.53%	8.38%	8.78%
5 TO 9 YEARS	7.18%	8.00%	8.39%
10 TO 14 YEARS	7.00%	7.34%	7.66%
15 TO 17 YEARS	5.08%	4.70%	4.69%
18 TO 20 YEARS	5.43%	4.88%	4.63%
21 TO 24 YEARS	6.14%	5.84%	5.48%
25 TO 29 YEARS	8.27%	8.29%	7.94%
30 TO 34 YEARS	6.57%	7.75%	7.77%
35 TO 39 YEARS	6.45%	7.38%	7.67%
40 TO 49 YEARS	15.63%	14.18%	14.06%
50 TO 59 YEARS	11.62%	10.29%	9.87%
60 TO 64 YEARS	4.50%	3.77%	3.52%
65 TO 69 YEARS	3.06%	3.10%	2.94%
70 TO 74 YEARS	2.13%	2.40%	2.49%
75+ YEARS	3.42%	3.71%	4.09%
MEDIAN AGE	32.58	31.66	31.56
AVERAGE AGE	34.23	33.45	33.26

DESCRIPTION	1.00 MILE RADIUS	3.00 MILE RADIUS	4.00 MILE RADIUS
1999 EST. FEMALE POP. BY AGE	5,075	24,695	83,137
UNDER 5 YEARS	7.21%	8.06%	8.39%
5 TO 9 YEARS	7.01%	7.79%	8.08%
10 TO 14 YEARS	6.56%	7.07%	7.23%
15 TO 17 YEARS	5.03%	4.62%	4.53%
18 TO 20 YEARS	5.08%	4.62%	4.41%
21 TO 24 YEARS	5.85%	5.67%	5.32%
25 TO 29 YEARS	8.02%	7.97%	7.68%
30 TO 34 YEARS	6.47%	7.47%	7.54%
35 TO 39 YEARS	6.10%	7.27%	7.54%
40 TO 49 YEARS	16.36%	14.46%	14.21%
50 TO 59 YEARS	11.89%	10.63%	10.19%
60 TO 64 YEARS	4.67%	3.84%	3.66%
65 TO 69 YEARS	3.16%	3.22%	3.16%
70 TO 74 YEARS	2.25%	2.68%	2.88%
75+ YEARS	4.34%	4.62%	5.20%
FEMALE MEDIAN AGE	34.05	32.80	32.90
FEMALE AVERAGE AGE	35.29	34.48	34.55
POPULATION BY HOUSEHOLD TYPE	9,387	45,421	149,584
FAMILY HOUSEHOLDS	93.19%	89.05%	89.39%
NON-FAMILY HOUSEHOLDS	6.23%	7.99%	8.75%
GROUP QUARTERS	0.59%	2.96%	1.86%
HOUSEHOLDS BY TYPE	2,948	14,495	48,721
SINGLE MALE	5.82%	7.53%	8.21%
SINGLE FEMALE	7.81%	9.43%	10.29%
MARRIED COUPLE	62.05%	55.26%	54.19%
OTHER FAMILY—MALE HEAD	5.50%	5.06%	4.82%
OTHER FAMILY—FEMALE HEAD	16.14%	19.31%	18.94%
NON FAMILY—MALE HEAD	1.80%	2.23%	12.29%
NON FAMILY—FEMALE HEAD	0.88%	1.19%	1.25%
POPULATION BY URBAN VS. RURAL	9,343	45,307	149,314
URBAN	100.00%	99.57%	99.32%
RURAL	0.00%	0.43%	0.68%

Exhibit 3A—Sample Demographic Report

Traffic Counts: Another criterion to consider is the traffic count for a location. Most strip shopping centers have recent auto traffic counts for the main streets surrounding their shopping center. Regional malls may have auto traffic counts for the parking lot, but will probably have customer counts at different locations inside the mall. You can use these counts to compare different locations, both within the city and within the same center.

If a strip shopping center doesn't have auto traffic counts, they can usually be obtained from the city or county planning department. If you are going into a strip shopping center or neighborhood center, look for the shopping center location that has a strong traffic count, but not necessarily the highest. Sometimes traffic congestion is a drawback to a location. If you are going into a mall location, try to find out what the traffic patterns are within the mall. If the mall does not have any information on customer traffic counts within the mall, a couple of hours observation on a Saturday afternoon will probably tell you where the higher traffic is.

Economic Condition of the Shopping Center: When comparing shopping centers, it is a really good idea to look at the overall development and condition of the shopping center. There are some ways to measure shopping centers:

- **Quality of anchor tenants:** Are the anchors doing well? Do they draw the right type of customer for your business? A very successful, well-located shopping center anchored with a warehouse food store and a discount variety store may not offer the best location for a high-end jewelry shop.

- **Quality of the other tenants:** Are there popular stores locating in the shopping center? Is there a good mix of a variety of merchandise? Do the other tenants contribute to your business, or compete with your business? Will the shoppers at the other stores in the center likely shop at your business?

- **Sales productivity:** Find out the average *sales per square foot* for the shopping center, and compare with other shopping centers. The sales productivity of the center is the number one indicator of how well the shops are performing. Sometimes, the leasing agents will release sales information on specific stores, or a category of stores. Try to find out as much as you can, and compare the information to other shopping centers, or compare it to averages in the appendix.

- **Average occupancy:** Is there a lot of vacancy? Have many stores have failed? What types of stores have failed? Have higher quality stores been replaced with lower quality? Have new tenants made significant investments into new stores?

- **Physical Condition of the Shopping Center:** Look at the condition of the parking lot. Has the asphalt been well maintained? Are the curbs painted? Are the pavement markings repainted frequently? Is the center attractive? Is it well landscaped? Go by the center after dark and see if the parking lot is well lit, and if the lighted signs are all on. Check the age of the shopping center.

- **Cleanliness:** If you are looking at an enclosed mall, is it clean? Are the restrooms and other amenities clean? Is the parking convenient?

- **Competition:** Is a new shopping center planned or under development? A visit to the local city or county planning department will pay off, and let you know if any competing shopping centers are coming. Most planning departments maintain a list of developments that are in various stages of planning or permits.

- If a new center just opened in the area, how did it affect the sales and occupancy of the older center? Is the market growing fast enough to absorb new competition, or will sales be split between competing stores and competing centers.

- **Temporary Tenant Program:** Does the shopping center have a specialty leasing program or other opportunities for you to consider? These programs are very valuable for starting a new retail business, and should be investigated. (See the section on Specialty Leasing).

- **Tenant Improvements:** Will the shopping center owner do some tenant improvement work? Usually, the leasing agent won't commit to this right up front, but just ask if the landlord has done any tenant improvement work for other tenants recently. If a landlord in one shopping center is more likely to help with the TI work, it may make a difference in your decision when comparing locations.

COMPARING SPACES WITHIN THE SHOPPING CENTER

After locating two or three possible shopping center locations, take a look at the actual spaces you are being offered within each shopping center. Often, there are opportunities in shopping centers that can only be found by talking to the mall management and leasing staff. There are owners of businesses who would like to sell, or there are company stores that would like to find a franchisee. Don't just walk or drive by a center and assume that there are no opportunities because there are no "For Lease" signs.

After finding out what locations in each shopping center are available for your consideration, make your decision after considering some of the following factors:

- **Visibility:** In a strip shopping center, the visibility of some spaces is blocked. Trees, perimeter buildings, bus stops, signs and other obstructions may block the motorists' view of a space in an outdoor center. In an enclosed mall, kiosks, mall directories, elevators or escalators, plants, and other things often block the view of a storefront.

- **Corner Locations:** The corner location is obviously the best because it has more visibility. In a strip shopping center, the end cap location is sought after by chain stores that want to have great visibility from the street. In an enclosed mall, the corner spaces on the center courts are high-rent locations, but there are usually in-line spaces close to a center court with visibility from two directions.

- **Traffic Patterns:** In any shopping center, there are traffic patterns. These are formed by the way the parking lot is laid out, or by the entrances to certain anchor stores, or the location of the food court, etc. In a mall, some anchor stores produce more foot traffic than others, but some produce a higher quality of cross-shopping customer, so consider all elements.

- **Side Locations:** These locations are down the hall, or around the corner from the main traffic areas. The traffic going by the space is less, but the rent is typically much lower, and these locations can be good for destination businesses, such as personal services.

- **Storefront Width:** Wide, shallow spaces are usually preferred over long, narrow spaces because the business has more storefront exposure.

- **Vacant Space Available:** Don't pass a shopping center by just because you don't see any vacancies available. If the center meets your overall selection criteria, visit with the management and leasing staff and see what spaces might be available or coming up. Frequently, the best space is not vacant. Perhaps there is a tenant on a short-term lease or a tenant planning to leave.

COMPARING SALES & RENT IN SHOPPING CENTERS

The following tables compare similar store categories in different types of shopping centers from a survey published by the Urban Land Institute.[1] A Super Regional Mall is typically about 1,000,000 SF in size of Gross Leasable Area. A Regional Mall is typically about 500,000 SF in GLA. A Community Shopping Center is about 150,000 SF and is not enclosed. A Neighborhood Shopping Center is about 60,000 SF, usually specializing in convenience goods.

The total rent includes both the minimum base rent, and overage or percentage rent, but does not include charges such as CAM.

Table 4.1 Super Regional Shopping Malls[2]

Tenant Classification	Median Sales PSF	Median Total Rent PSF
Jewelry	$852.21	$66.42
Women's Wear	250.60	22.22
Family Shoes	263.90	23.00
Cards & Gifts	237.53	26.00
Family Wear	343.90	25.00
Decorative Accessories	319.42	34.22

Table 4.2 Regional Shopping Malls[3]

Tenant Classification	Median Sales PSF	Median Total Rent PSF
Jewelry	$837.83	$50.17
Women's Wear	294.73	25.00

1. ULI-the Urban Land Institute, *Dollars & Cents of Shopping Centers: 2002.* Washington, D.C.: ULI-the Urban Land Institute.
2. *Dollars & Cents of Shopping Centers: 2002,* pages 44–45.
3. *Dollars & Cents of Shopping Centers,* page 102

Tenant Classification	Median Sales PSF	Median Total Rent PSF
Family Shoes	259.09	19.00
Cards & Gifts	202.91	19.00
Family Wear	342.98	18.03
Decorative Accessories	317.97	32.26

Table 4.3 Community Shopping Centers[4]

Tenant Classification	Median Sales PSF	Median Total Rent PSF
Jewelry	$452.97	$20.48
Women's Wear	178.84	13.03
Family Shoes	176.35	14.11
Cards & Gifts	141.29	13.00
Family Wear	206.69	12.00
Cosmetics/Beauty Supplies	319.20	18.00

Table 4.4 Neighborhood Shopping Centers[5]

Tenant Classification	Median Sales PSF	Median Total Rent PSF
Jewelry	$432.54	$15.66
Cards & Gifts	228.55	12.65
Dry Cleaner	166.72	15.36
Women's Hair Salon	151.91	11.90
Videotape Rentals	86.66	12.60
Nail Salon	82.50	14.03

---

4. *Dollars & Cents of Shopping Centers*, page 149
5. *Dollars & Cents of Shopping Centers*, page 215

The above charts show that the rent is usually in direct proportion to the size of the shopping center and the level of sales. The average rent for a Jewelry Store, for example, in a neighborhood center is about ¼ of a super regional mall, but the sales are about half. You have to decide if you'd rather pay the extra rent money for the higher sales, but in most cases it is more than worth the price.

As an example, consider a jewelry store of 1,000 SF. In a super regional mall the rent is $66,620 per year and the sales are $852,210. Your gross sales after rent are $785,590.

Contrast that with a shop in a neighborhood center: your rent would be much less at $15,660 per year, but your sales would be $432,540. Your gross sales after rent are $416,880. Would you rather pay the higher rent if you could get the higher sales?

4

APPLYING TO LEASE A SPACE IN A SHOPPING CENTER

✦

How to Get Them to Call You Back

Trying to rent space in a shopping center can be frustrating. Knowing how to approach the leasing agent and how to make a proper application can improve your chances of getting the best space at the best terms.

INQUIRING ABOUT LEASING SPACE IN A SHOPPING CENTER

Anyone who has tried to inquire about leasing a space in a busy and successful shopping center has found how difficult it is to actually get through to someone who can answer questions and give them information on leasing a space. Why? As soon as a caller asks a question that shows he/she is unprepared and unqualified to lease a space, the leasing agent or property manager knows the odds are that the caller will probably never lease a space, and the call falls to the bottom of the priority list.

The first mistake that many novice business owners make is to find a vacancy in a shopping center they might be interested in and then calling the leasing agent and asking to "go take a look at it"—like it's a used car or something.

The second mistake that most novices make is to call the management office for the shopping center and ask, "How much does it cost to rent a space there?"

With this approach, it is doubtful that they will actually get to talk to anyone past the receptionist, or they will end up leaving a voice mail message that probably won't be returned.

To avoid this frustration, learn how to talk to leasing agents.

THE FIRST DUMB QUESTION: "CAN I LOOK AT THE SPACE?"

Most people make the mistake of inquiring about vacant spaces in a shopping center the way they would about a vacant house or apartment for rent, which is probably the only experience they have ever had with renting or leasing any real estate. When someone is ready to move out of an apartment or rented house, they simply call the landlord and give 30 days notice and then move out. The landlord or leasing agent posts a "for rent" sign in the yard or an ad in the paper and waits for someone to drive by or call. When the call comes, the leasing agent is eager to take the call and rent the unit as quickly as possible.

It doesn't work that way in a shopping center. Most of the occupants of a shopping center are businesses who are on leases extending over several years. Typically, when a vacancy occurs, it didn't just "happen" in the last 30 days. If a tenant has reached the end of its lease term, the leasing agent or property manager knows well in advance if the tenant is not going to stay. Likewise, if a tenant's business is failing and is in danger of going out of business, the property manager knows well in advance. By the time the passer-by sees a vacant space appear in a busy shopping center, it is a good bet that the property manager and leasing agents have been working on finding a new tenant for that space for several months. So, when you call up and say, "Hey, I just saw a vacancy in your shopping center and would like to take a look at it," they will just roll their eyes. Or, more likely, they won't return your call.

Perhaps the leasing agent has been working on a big new store to come into the shopping center for the past year, and the deal involves consolidating three smaller spaces together. She has to relocate one tenant, terminate a lease with one other tenant, and negotiate a remodel for a third tenant. Whew! That is a lot of work and she's been working on this for about a year. Finally, the deal is coming together and the tenant who is leaving closes its doors. Then she gets your call and you want to go look at the inside of the space that you just noticed was vacant. She's not going to spend a lot of time with you.

THE SECOND DUMB QUESTION: "HOW MUCH DOES IT COST?"

Again, most people approach shopping center leasing in the same manner they would a residential unit. They assume that all the spaces in the shopping center pay the same rent, or the same rent per square foot. When they rented their first apartment, they were told that plan "A" rented for $500 a month and plan "B", with 65 more square feet, rented for $550 per month. So, they call up a shopping center management office and ask how much it costs to lease a space. Once again, they probably won't get through, or their message won't be returned. Like the caller who wants to look at a vacant space, they have tipped off the leasing agent that they are unqualified and unprepared.

Most novice people are surprised to learn that rental rates in a shopping center vary widely. The rental rates are complex and there is no 'quoted rental rate'. Rates vary depending on the type of business use, the location in the center, how much the landlord is putting into the space, and the sales of the tenant. So, when you ask how much the rent is, you have just skipped all of the stuff in the middle of your business plan, and by doing so, you've unknowingly told the leasing agent that you are not a qualified prospect.

The time to talk about rent is after you have the leasing agent or property manager interested in your store concept, when they are trying to get you to lease a space in their center.

TO GET A LEASING AGENT OR PROPERTY MANAGER TO CALL YOU BACK:

- Don't ask about a particular space, even if you saw a space and it triggered your interest, and don't ask to go look at the inside of it.

- Don't ask how much it costs to rent a space.

- Instead, do tell the agent about your business or prospective business and the type of store you are planning to open.

- Then, ask if you can make an appointment to discuss your business plan.

TELL THE AGENT ABOUT YOUR BUSINESS

Approach the leasing agent as a sales prospect. Get the agent interested in what you can offer his shopping center. Do this by talking about your business or prospective business in a manner that opens the door for further conversation.

Let's say you call the management office for a shopping center and leave a message for the leasing agent:

"I have developed a new retail store concept that is fresh, new and different, and would fit in nicely with the tenant mix of your shopping center. I have some solid financing in place, and I'm starting to talk to leasing agents of retail properties similar to yours to discuss possible locations. I'd like to set up a time when I can come in and show you what I'm developing."

Do you think you'll get a call back with this type of message?

When you get to the meeting with the leasing agent, remember that you are trying to sell them on you and your prospective retail store. Resist the temptation to ask about that small store that just became vacant near center court, even if you are dying to find out if it's available. Let the leasing agent bring it up. When the conversation gets around to some specifics, such as store size, the agent will eventually pull out a leasing plan and will soon tell you what is available in the center. Remember not to get too specific with questions about any particular space, and don't ask to go see a space yet. Your goal of this first contact is to get them interested in you and your prospective business. Don't fast forward to any specifics until you have sold them on your store concept.

Also, don't bring up the rent at this point. The leasing agent may bring it up and throw a high rent number at you just to see how qualified you are. If that happens, say something like, "That's probably a little high, but we can talk about that later." Let the agent know that you are fully prepared to pay a reasonable rent if you get the deal you want, and if their shopping center has the right location for you and can produce the type of traffic you are looking for. Tell them you'll pay twice that if you can do business at their center. If you have already done your research, you won't be surprised about the rent, and you'll know going in that the rent is highly negotiable.

To be able to have such a discussion with a leasing agent, of course, means that you do have a viable store concept and that you have prepared a business plan and are ready to discuss a location that meets your requirements. Don't call the leasing agent until you are ready. And if your business plan or store concept does not generate enthusiasm, go back to the drawing board. You aren't going to rent any space until they believe in your plan. Leasing agents do not like to lease space in shopping centers to tenants who are just going to fail in a short time.

After you have established a rapport with the leasing agent, and you have decided on a specific location that you'd like to pursue go back for a second or third meeting with the leasing agent and start discussing the terms of the lease, including the rent. Before negotiating the lease terms and rent, you should carefully review the sections on shopping center leases in this book. There is far more to negotiate than just the rent.

YOUR BUSINESS PLAN

There are many good books available on how to write a business plan for a new business. Some colleges and local governments have resources to help you get started. The written business plan can be a very simple outline of your business plans, or it can be a long, detailed package. For most shopping center managers and leasing agents, a simple plan works just fine. It should include the following elements.

Financial Statement

The business plan includes a complete and accurate financial statement on the tenant entity. If you were a start-up small business, that usually means the tenant entity will be you, so the financial statement would be your personal financial statement. If you have a company that has been in business for a few years, the tenant entity might be the company, with your name on the lease as a lease guarantor. In that case, you would need to include financial statements on your company as well as your personal financial statement.

Balance Sheet: This is a list of your assets and your liabilities, and your net worth. Your net worth is the value of your total assets (what you own) less the value of your total liabilities (what you owe). The shopping center manager will want to see if your net worth is sufficient to support the new business—if you have enough capital to properly fund the business and support it in the critical early months and years.

Don't overstate your assets to puff up your net income, and don't leave out some liabilities or fail to show the accurate amounts. Your credibility will be seriously harmed, reducing your chances to get your business started. It is always better to be accurate and truthful when showing the values of your assets and liabilities.

Income Statement: If you have an existing business, this is a statement of your income from your operations. If you are a wage earner, you might just include the last year or two of income tax returns to show how much money you have earned. In the case of a business, the operating statement is usually for the last full year and the most recent year to date statement. The operating statement should show income from all sources, and expenses. Your net income from the business for the period shown is the income less the expenses.

If you are planning a start-up business and have not yet operated, you will need to make up a *pro forma income statement*. This is an estimate of future income and expenses and an estimated net income from operations. This will be a critical document in the business plan. Your forecasted income must be supported by your research.

Estimating Retail Sales: If you are starting a retail or service business, you will need to estimate your sales to be able to make a pro forma income statement. There are different ways to estimate sales. Here are some guidelines:

- Find out what other similar stores are doing in your area. If you are attempting to lease space in shopping centers, sometimes the shopping center manager or leasing agent will tell you what the average sales are for some stores similar to yours. Use those averages to estimate your sales. If you are opening a new restaurant in a mall food court, for example, the shopping center manager should be able to give you the average sales for similar restaurants in the food court.

- Use industry publications. In the shopping center industry, there is a publication called "Dollars & Cents of Shopping Centers" published by the Urban Land Institute every two years. They research records from many shopping centers in all regions of the country and categorize the results by type of center and type of tenant. The results show the median for different types of businesses. It also shows the results for small independent businesses and large chain stores.

- Use your suppliers. They are selling merchandise to stores like yours, and they can help you estimate your sales based on their experience.

Inventory Levels

If you are planning a retail store, your sales estimate must be supported by your forecasted inventory. If you don't have it on the shelf you can't sell it. Don't make the mistake of planning to buy $25,000 worth of inventory to open the business, and then plan for sales of $50,000 per month. How is that possible?

Average Turn Over Ratio: Find out what the average turnover of your inventory will be for your type of business. Hopefully, you or someone else has some experience in the type of retail store you are opening, and knows what the average turnover is for the different types of products. The turnover ratio varies for different types of businesses. Some may only turn their inventory 2 or 3 times a year, while a grocery store turns inventory more than 52 times a year.

Use the turnover ratio to estimate sales. Once you know your average turnover, you can predict your sales. If the average for your store is 4 times per year, and you are planning to have an average of $100,000 in inventory, your sales can be estimated at $400,000 per year. Or, looking at it the other way, if you want sales of $400,000 per year, and you know the average turn over is 4 times per year, you need to plan to have an average inventory of $100,000.

Equipment & Capital Costs

Your business plan should include an estimate of the costs to establish your business. These costs include the cost of the Tenant Improvements to the leased space, and also the cost of Furniture, Fixtures and Equipment that will be necessary to operate your business.

Estimates and descriptions of actual costs should be included, as well as the sources of funding to capitalize the investment. If you are going to be asking the landlord for a tenant allowance to assist with the improvements to your space, you must have some idea of what these improvements are going to cost.

Equipment suppliers will usually assist with a list of needed equipment and prices. Tenant Improvement contractors can look at your plans for a store and give you a budget estimate of what it will cost to make the improvements.[1]

Description of Business

The business plan should include a description of the type of business you are proposing to bring to the shopping center. If you have an existing business, this could be easily done with photographs and descriptions of your existing store. If you have a restaurant, for example, you might include the menu or other information. Many times, a small business has enjoyed a write-up or an editorial in a magazine or newspaper, and copies of these might be included. If you have done a lot of print advertising, copies of the ads could be included in the package.

If yours is a start-up business, you can include photos of some of the products you will be selling. Sometimes, the business plan will include some copies of catalog cuts from suppliers to show the types of inventory that will be carried.

Brand names are important, along with price points. You should show how you are going to compete: price, selection, or service. Describe your niche in the market, and how you will attempt to gain customers.

Personal Information

The business plan usually includes some information on the owners/principals of the business. A resume of experience on each one, their photos, and any industry-related training or education is usually very helpful to show the background and ability of the owners.

 The business plan should show the type of business you want to open, and the financial information to show that it will be successful. This requires some research and time, but it is time well spent. A properly researched business plan not only impresses the leasing agent, but also gives you a giant leg up on improving your chances for success.

---

1.   See Chapter on Tenant Improvements

5

SPECIALTY LEASING

✦

Take Advantage of the Temporary Tenant Program

If you are considering a retail location for a start-up business, but funds are limited, consider a Specialty Leasing program. Specialty Leasing is temporary retailing from a cart or kiosk, or the temporary rental of a vacant storefront space.

All Regional Malls and most Lifestyle Centers have a Specialty Leasing program. In many cases, there is a Specialty Leasing manager who works exclusively with short term, temporary, and specialty types of retail tenants. These shopping centers use the program to generate income and bring new retailers into the center that otherwise wouldn't have a chance to get started.

Some of the carts and kiosks are rented on a temporary basis for seasonal periods, such as the Christmas season, and these retailers bring unique and interesting products to add to the merchandise mix, which creates interest in the common areas, and stimulates shopper activity.

In some cases, a Specialty Leasing program is also used to fill otherwise-vacant storefront locations while waiting for a permanent leasing prospect. This is a good opportunity for a start-up or temporary business to open a retail store, especially for a seasonal use. It is also a good opportunity to try out a new retail business with a limited capital investment or long-term lease commitment.

CARTS AND KIOSKS

Portable merchandising units are used in most Regional Malls in the common areas of the shopping centers. They are also often seen in Lifestyle Centers and other shopping centers with common walking areas. These retail-merchandising units (RMU) had their beginning as wagon-wheeled pushcarts, and the term "cart" has become a generic term. These units are on casters and easily moved about the center. Most are elaborately designed with quality finishes and a design that matches the shopping center's amenities. Carts are designed to display product or information on all four sides, and the attendant is positioned on the outside of the cart. There is usually a separate cash-wrap stand and a stool for the attendant's use.

A kiosk, on the other hand, is a larger unit that is not portable. The kiosk is designed with an open space in the middle for the attendants, with counter displays around the perimeter. Kiosks range in size from 10' to 15' wide and 10' to 20' long. Kiosks are often rented on a permanent basis with long-term leases. Some kiosks are brought in and assembled for a short-term use, such as during the Christmas season.

Carts and short-term kiosks are typically rented month-to-month, or for a short term, such as for the Christmas shopping season. However, many cart tenants rent them for several months at a time on a year-round basis.

Rent Guidelines for Carts & Kiosks:

The rent for a cart or temporary kiosk varies depending on the traffic and sales activity in the shopping center. In a middle market shopping center, the base rent for non-Holiday seasons can be very reasonable, under $1,000 per month. In a large urban shopping center with high volumes of traffic and sales, the rent is much more. A typical cart lease deal would include a monthly base rent and a monthly percentage rental of around 12% to 15%, with a natural breakpoint[1]. That may seem high, but consider that a typical mall store, which pays 5% to 8% percentage rent, also pays for CAM, taxes, insurance, utilities, and other occupancy costs. With a cart or kiosk, the landlord supplies the electricity, and does not usually charge the tenant for the additional expenses of CAM, Real Estate

---

1.   See the chapter on Percentage Rent for an explanation of how percentage rent is calculated.

Taxes, Insurance and other charges. If these charges or any other charges are added to the base rent, then the percentage rent should be adjusted so the tenant is paying a maximum of 12% to 15% of sales in total occupancy charges.

The square footage rent for a permanent kiosk is high, typically over $100 PSF. Many of these kiosks are used for retail items such as jewelry and sunglasses, which generate high sales and pay high rent.

Location: Choosing the right location for a cart or kiosk is important. Some areas of enclosed malls have higher foot traffic than other areas, and some malls have more traffic than other malls. Most carts offer impulse items and so sales are directly related to traffic. A good idea would be for the business owner to visit several locations and several malls to observe traffic before deciding on a location. Many malls have sophisticated equipment that counts pedestrian traffic at mall entrances and other locations. Ask if these numbers are available and compare traffic counts at different locations.

Carts and kiosks are a good arrangement for a you if you have limited capital or an unproven business. It is a low-cost way to test the market, to test a product, to incubate a new business concept, or to operate a short-term business for a peak selling season.

The benefits of renting a cart or kiosk:

- **Start up costs are lower**
- **Operating costs are lower**
- **Short lease commitment, typically month-to-month**
- **Opportunity to test a new product or new concept**
- **Opportunity to operate a 'branch office'**
- **Work well for lead-generation for real estate brokers, mortgage brokers, vacations and time-share sales, home improvement services, and other types of non-retail use**

IN-LINE MALL SPACE

It is possible to rent in-line mall space in a Regional Mall on a low-cost basis. Most malls have some vacant *second-generation spaces*[2]—even the busiest malls. It typically takes several months or years to lease a vacant mall space to a national retail tenant because most national retailers are making plans for new stores at least two or three years out. Most of the time, mall space just doesn't lease quickly. This provides an opportunity for the start-up retail business owner to obtain some space at a fraction of the rent and capital investment normally paid for a long-term lease.

Usually, the temporary leasing of vacant in-line space falls under the Specialty Leasing program. Temporary tenants who rent vacant mall space are either renting it for a short time period, or are trying to develop a business.

The vacant spaces used in a Specialty Leasing program are those referred to as *second-generation* spaces. This refers to spaces that have been built out by a previous tenant, where the tenant vacated and left usable improvements behind.

Seasonal Tenants: There are several types of tenants that lease vacant spaces in malls and shopping centers on a short-term, seasonal basis: Toy stores, Halloween stores, Christmas decoration stores, Calendar stores, etc. Many national retailers operate seasonal stores that are only open 2 or 3 months of the year. They scout out locations, usually for the fourth quarter Holiday season, throughout the country and open and operate dozens to hundreds of temporary stores.

This same opportunity is available to you. You don't have to sign a long-term lease for a seasonal store. If you can find a fairly decent built-out space in a mall with good traffic, there is opportunity to open a store for the busy Holiday season.

Rent for a seasonal tenant is based on whatever the malls can get—there is seldom a set guideline. For a known product such as Calendars, there is probably some sales history, and the retailer can usually make a reasonable estimate on what the store will do, and agree to pay a rent based on a percentage of the estimated sales.

---

2.   See Chapter on Tenant Improvements for description of "Second-Generation Space".

A start-up business with no sales history has a more difficult time of determining what rent can be paid and still show a profit. Try to find out what any similar seasonal stores have done in the same mall in prior years. Estimate the sales based on the inventory that will be stocked in the store (if it's not on the shelf, it can't be sold). Not every item will be sold, of course, and you will have to take steep mark downs at the end of the season to get rid of excess merchandise.

In-Line Rent: Expect to pay a base rent and a percentage of sales. You might also be charged for some CAM or Marketing Fund expenses, so make sure you look at the total rent bill, not just the base rent[3].

Overage Rent: For a short-term rental it is very important to get the percentage rent clause worded in the lease so that the percentage rent is paid on the full term of the occupancy, **not** on a monthly basis[4]. This is a pitfall to avoid, and you can save substantially on the rent.

For example, say you are opening a temporary store in a mall to sell Christmas decorations and you plan to be open from October 1st through January 15th. Assume $80,000 in sales for the season. The sales pattern might look something like this: $8,000 in October, $16,000 in November, $48,000 in December, and $8,000 in January (at half-price). If your rent were, say, $3,000 per month and 10% of sales over $30,000 *per month*, you would pay rent as follows:

Example of total rent paid with a *monthly* breakpoint:

Month	Base Rent	Sales	Overage Rent	Total Rent Paid
October:	$3,000	$8,000	None	$3,000
November:	$3,000	$16,000	None	$3,000
December:	$3,000	$48,000	$1,800	$4,800
January	$1,500	$8,000	None	$1,500
				$12,300

The total rent paid with a ***monthly breakpoint*** percentage rent formula is
$12,300.

---

3.   See chapters on CAM and other lease expenses.
4.   See Overage Rent chapter for a full explanation of how Overage Rent works.

Now consider the same example with rent of $3,000 per month and 10% of sales over a natural breakpoint for the ***entire term*** of the lease.[5] The **total base rent is $10,500** for the 3 ½ month term, so the percentage rent breakpoint would be $105,000 for the entire term.

Example of total rent paid for the same lease, with a *term* breakpoint:

Month	Base Rent	Sales	Overage Rent	Total Rent Paid
October:	$3,000	$8,000		$3,000
November:	$3,000	$16,000		$3,000
December:	$3,000	$48,000		$3,000
January	$1,500	$8,000		$1,500
Total	**$10,500**	**$80,000**	**None**	**$10,500**

The total rent paid with a ***term breakpoint*** percentage rent formula is **$10,500**

In this example, no percentage rent would be due since the total sales of $80,000 are below the $105,000 breakpoint, thus **saving $1,800 in rent**. With just a simple change in the lease provision for percentage rent you saved a lot of money that goes directly into your pocket. Will leasing agents agree to this? Yes, but the standard lease form will usually provide for a monthly breakpoint, so *you have to ask for it.*

---

5.   See Chapter on Percentage Rent for description of "Natural Breakpoint".

Whenever you are renting a space for a short term, try to get the percentage rent computed over the entire term so you can average the high and low sales months. If you accept the standard base rent/percentage rent formula on a monthly basis, you will likely pay percentage rent in the high sales month.

MONTH-TO-MONTH TEMPORARY TENANTS

In addition to short-term temporary tenancies, there are opportunities for Specialty Leasing on a longer-term basis, such year and month-to-month agreements. Most Specialty Leasing programs will lease vacant mall space to a "temporary tenant" for an indefinite time, as long as the space is not leased to a long-term tenant at full rent. This is a great opportunity for a start-up business to obtain a mall space at a fraction of the rent that would have to be paid on a permanent lease.

Incubator Deals: You can incubate a business under a short-term lease. The lower rent payments and lower overhead give the owner some breathing room to get the business established and get the sales up high enough to warrant a long-term commitment. This may be a year, or even two years. Many malls have "temporary tenants" who have been in business for years on a month-to-month agreement at a fraction of the rent that it would cost to lease the space permanently.

The downside to this arrangement, of course, is that the tenant could lose the space at any time. If the mall were able to find a prospective tenant for the space, the temporary tenant would get a 30-day or 60-day notice to move out. So a short-term tenancy only works when the owner is taking advantage of a situation. It typically won't work for a long time.

Beware of a long-term investment on a short-term lease. Occasionally, when an older mall is struggling with sales losses and loss of market share, vacancies will start to appear and the mall managers will attempt to fill the vacancies with short-term leases. They will lease otherwise vacant space to a start-up business on a low monthly rent just to have a store open and operating. If there is a shortage of national tenants to fill space, the mall may continue operating in this manner while the owners of the property decide what to do with the shopping center. If and when a redevelopment of the shopping center is started, and new retail tenants are found to lease space, the local tenants that have been operating on a "temporary" status (sometimes for several years) are given the boot. Many of these tenants have invested in their stores by this time, made improvements, invested in inventory and fixtures, and are supporting themselves with the business, so they are shocked and outraged that they would be kicked out to make way for a higher rent paying national tenant. Somewhere they failed to realize the situation they were in. It can be dangerous to invest in a retail store for an open-ended, long term without a lease—your business is only 30 days away from being moved into your garage.

This same thing happens when the economy is down. More retail vacancies appear and the mall managers are all too happy to lease you a space at a low rent. But when the economy starts to recover (after you have hung on through the tough times), the national retailers start building new stores again, and the "temporary tenant" loses his space.

Notwithstanding these risks, however, you can still take advantage of the temporary tenant situation; you just can't plan on it lasting forever. The idea is to find a space that has been previously built out that will work for the business, lease it on a short-term basis and "see how it goes". As the business sales start to increases, the business owner can invest more money into inventory instead of rent, and continue to grow the business. Within a short time, say around a year to two years, the business will either be achieving the average sales levels needed to stay viable, or it won't. If the business is viable, and the owner wants to keep the business open long-term, then it's time to talk to the mall's leasing agents about a long-term lease. On the other hand, if the business is only producing at a below-average sales pace, the owner can decide to stay on a temporary status basis, but the owner must understand that temporary means temporary. It will come to an end someday.

Rent for In-Line Spaces: If you are renting an in-line space on an indefinite temporary period, or for up to a year, you should try to bargain for a low rent. Sell the mall on the *incubator* concept, that you are trying to get a new store developed and that when the business is fully developed, you will pay higher rents. Can you get an in-line store for a thousand dollars a month? Five hundred? Yes, it depends on the location and the circumstances. Many times, you can get into a space on a percentage rent only basis.

If you are paying a standard base rent and overage rent, try to avoid the overage rent computed on a monthly basis. Even if it is a month-to-month lease, try to negotiate to have the percentage rent calculated on at least a quarterly basis, to give you an opportunity to average some of the high and low sales months. A long-term lease computes percentage rent on an annual basis.[6]

Most of the time, the mall will ask the temporary tenant to pay some of the CAM costs and the Marketing Fund. This is only fair, since the tenant will be using some of the services of the mall, and enjoying the occupancy in the mall. But remember to look at the total rent bill, and not just the base rent when considering how much your total occupancy charge will be, and don't go over the range of 12% to 15% of total sales, for most retail businesses.

Tenant Improvements: When leasing an in-line mall space on a "temporary" basis, it doesn't make any sense to invest a lot of money in capital improvements to the space. If you are a month-to-month tenant, the landlord (or you) can terminate the lease anytime with 30 days notice. Don't forget that this is a two-way street—realize the landlord can terminate the lease as easily as you can.

However, you must be willing to invest some money into a store or the business will never get off the ground. A decent sign is important, although the sign does not have to be an expensive internally lit sign. A good sign shop can make an inexpensive 3-dimensional lettered sign with a little creative design. Lighting is also extremely important. If the prior tenant took all the display lighting, such as track lights and spotlights, they will have to be reinstalled. Don't attempt to skimp on lighting and try to get by with just fluorescent lights—your business will suffer.

Make sure the floor covering is adequate and doesn't detract from your merchandise. Used display equipment and fixtures can save money, and some creativity goes a long way in adapting some inexpensive items, such as wooden ladders, as display equipment. However, be careful not to junk up the store with a bunch of mismatched cabinets and fixtures. If you are attempting to develop a quality business in a quality shopping center, you don't want your store to look like a flea market or a thrift store. Some investment will be necessary, but with some creativity you can do it for a fraction of the cost of building a new store.

If you can, try to get the landlord to make some of the improvements to the space, if any are needed. If you are agreeing to a 6-month or longer lease, it is not unreasonable to ask the landlord to contribute a month's worth of rent towards improvements to the space, especially if the improvements will improve your chances of success and give the mall a better-looking tenant.

---

6.   See previous examples on percentage rent in this chapter.

6

BASE RENT

✦

Shopping Centers are NOT a Level Playing Field

Base Rent is the basic rental payment, usually due monthly. Sometimes Base Rent is referred to as Minimum Rent or Base Minimum Rent. The word *minimum* refers to leases that have a Base Minimum Rent and an Overage Rent. The Minimum Rent is the minimum the tenant will pay—the Overage Rent is in addition to the Minimum Rent.

In most malls, the base rent and other costs are quoted as an annual rent, such as $24 per square foot. In most strip centers, the rent and other costs are most often quoted as a monthly rent, such as $2 per square foot. But sometimes, leasing agents and shopping center managers will quote either monthly or annual costs for any type of shopping center.

NET RENT

In a shopping center lease, the tenants normally pay for the common area costs of operating the center (CAM), as well as the allocation of real estate taxes (RET) and property insurance (INS) for the space. This is sometimes referred to as a "triple net lease", meaning that the base rent is net of CAM, RET and INS. The landlord receives the net rent and passes through the additional expenses associated with the real estate investment to the tenant.

If you are like most business owners, you typically refer to "rent" as the amount of the check you have to pay to the landlord on the first of each month. Be careful with the terminology. When a leasing agent or property manager speaks of "rent", the agent is usually talking about the Base Rent. Believe it or not, many tenants sign a lease without fully understanding the amount of the monthly check they will have to pay. In many enclosed malls, the costs of CAM, Real Estate Taxes, and Insurance can be almost as much, or more than the rent.

For the purposes here, the term "rent" will refer to Base Rent or Minimum Rent.

HOW MUCH IS THE RENT?

The first thing you may want to ask a leasing agent is, "How much is the rent?" To an experienced leasing agent, this means that the person asking doesn't understand the relationship between rent and sales. A good answer to this question would be, "If you could sell half a million dollars of your products, how much rent would you be willing to pay?"

In shopping centers, there is seldom any quoted rent price on a specific space. Rent is negotiable. Sometimes there is a budgeted number that the leasing agent feels might be obtainable, or there might be a rent number that the landlord needs to get, but the rent rates vary widely by the type of tenant, the size of the space, the location within the shopping center, the adjacent tenants, and other factors. In general, tenants who sell more pay more rent.

A better approach would be to inquire about the sales productivity of the center—what are the average sales of tenants similar to the business owner's store. If unsure about current market rates, one might ask the agent for a range of rental rates for a small space for local tenants.

The leasing agent will quote you a high rent. One leasing agent said he quotes a rent higher than he expects to get, just to see if the prospective tenant knows what he is doing. Other leasing agents always start high, knowing that in most cases they will come down. Don't go for any rate offered by a leasing agent until you have exhausted every attempt to get the rate you want and can afford.

The base rent is always, always, always negotiable, so negotiate for a deal. Try to figure out what the store will do in sales, and compute your rent and other occupancy costs based on what you can afford to pay. Make the rent fit within your business plan—don't make your business plan fit the rent the leasing agent quotes. Also, the rent should be based on your total *occupancy costs*, being careful to stay within a healthy range of less than 15%.

OCCUPANCY COSTS & OCCUPANCY COST RATIOS

The Base Rent must be considered with the other costs of tenancy that the tenant will pay. Here is an example of the types of charges a tenant might expect in a Regional Mall (although the actual costs vary widely):

ITEM	ANNUAL COST
Base Rent	$20 Per Square Foot
Common Area Maintenance	$10 Per Square Foot
Real Estate Taxes	$2 Per Square Foot
Marketing Fund	$2 Per Square Foot
Property Insurance	$0.50 Per Square Foot
Total	$34.50 PSF

Sometimes, a tenant might also pay air conditioning charges, trash charges, or utility charges to the landlord as well, but these charges are more along the lines of utilities than "rent".

If the average sales of the shopping center for the types of store that you are considering are $300 Per Square Foot per year, it is easy to calculate an *Occupancy Cost Ratio* for the average tenant of **11.5%.** Divide the total occupancy costs by the total sales to obtain the ratio—in this example, $34.50/$300 = .115, or 11.5%.

An 11.5% ratio should be fairly healthy for most tenants with an average margin on their sales of goods. Most shopping center managers feel like an occupancy cost ratio below 15% is probably okay and the tenant should be making a profit from the store. An occupancy cost ratio above 15% usually means the tenant is not making a profit, and a ratio going up to or above 20% is usually a sign that the tenant is losing money.

There are exceptions to these rules of thumb, such as with vending machines, amusement games and other similar businesses with low costs of goods sold. But for a typical retail or service business, the 15% ratio should be the uppermost they should consider. A good target is 11% to 13% for a new store.

Now you know the answer to the question, "How much is the rent?" The rent is what the business can afford to pay, based on the business sales forecast. If the forecast is based on inventory levels, market conditions, and the average of the shopping center location, the rent is a function of the sales.

If the occupancy cost ratio is too high, you have to either increase the sales or lower the rent and other charges. If you have done a good job forecasting your sales, then you need to get a lower rent. That's where you start negotiating.

FREE RENT

Is it possible to negotiate free rent in a shopping center? Sure, it might make sense for a tenant to have a rent free time for a few months of a new lease. This gives the tenant some time to get a store open and build up some business before taking on the big rent payments. A free rent period is also occasionally offered to help the tenant with some of the *Tenant Improvement* costs incurred to get the space ready and the store open.

Free rent means the landlord will have no large cash investment in the tenant's business, so there is less risk for the landlord. If you can afford your own tenant improvement costs, a free rent period at the commencement of the lease may be beneficial.

If your lease has an overage rent provision, make sure that the overage rent is also waived during the free rent period, not just the base rent. In most cases, you will still have to pay the other additional charges, such as CAM and RET, during a 'free rent' period.

PERCENTAGE RENT

Like a free rent period, occasionally a deal can be negotiated for a period of percentage rent in the first months of a shopping center lease. Again, this is a good plan to help a business get started without having some high rent payments.

Most small businesses are undercapitalized. With a Percentage Rent period, you can have some breathing room to get a business started. There is less chance of the business failing in the first critical months.

If you can combine a free rent period with a percentage rent period, you have a great chance to get a running start. But don't get used to it—the full rent is due someday.

Also, watch out for the double payment in the month that you switch from percentage rent to base rent. Percentage rent is paid in arrears; after the sales are made you pay a percent to the landlord, usually around the middle of the following month. Base rent is paid in advance, on the first of the month. So if you were switching from percentage rent to base rent in the month of May, you would be liable for paying the percentage rent on sales made in April, plus the base rent for the month of May. This trips up a lot of tenants. Plan for it.

STEP RENT

A shopping center lease is usually for a relatively long term. For that reason, there will almost always be some type of rent accelerator built into the lease. Most landlords (and tenants) prefer a stepped rent, where the Base Rent increases periodically over the lease term.

A typical 10-year lease would have a 3-4-3 step formula: the rent is level for 3 years, then increases for 4 years, then increases a second time for the final three years. A typical deal might be $20 PSF for 3 years, $22 PSF for 4 years, and $24 PSF for 3 years.

It is not unusual to find two rent steps on a 5-year lease. Occasionally there are rent steps every year during the term. But don't agree to higher rent steps than you can afford. If your rent starts at $15 and goes up $1 a year for five years, that is a 33% increase in rent in a 5-year period, probably much higher than a normal store's sales would increase during the same time period.

CONSUMER PRICE INDEX ADJUSTMENTS (CPI)

Some landlords have a standard CPI adjustment for the Base Rent in the lease. In this lease provision, the Base Rent is increased annually by a percentage increase based on a CPI Index. Sometimes the CPI increase is automatic every year, and sometimes the CPI clause is tied to overage rent—if the tenant is not paying overage rent at some future date, the CPI clause kicks in. Some landlords like to ask for both a stepped rent and a CPI increase.

Almost all tenants successfully negotiate out of the CPI clause, especially if there are some built-in steps in the base rent. Get the CPI clause deleted for the base rent.

However, the marketing fund payments the tenant makes are usually tied to CPI increases and this is probably reasonable. Most tenants agree to a CPI adjustment in the Marketing Fund so it increases gradually over the life of the lease. However, the typical shopping center lease requires the landlord to contribute a certain amount each year as well. If there is a CPI for the tenant, there probably should be one for the landlord's contribution as well. A strong marketing fund helps the shopping center, and benefits both the tenant and the landlord.

OTHER RENT INCREASES

Most shopping center leases have provisions to raise the tenant's rent if some future event happens; such as adding a new department store, remodeling the shopping center, etc. Try to get these provisions deleted.

NEGOTIATING BASE RENT

☑ Base Rent is always negotiable. Don't ever accept what the leasing agent offers. Use your business plan to establish your base rent and negotiate from there.

☑ Keep your occupancy costs well below 15% of estimated sales (for most businesses). Don't sign up for rent that is going to put you in over your head.

☑ When possible, negotiate for a free rent period and/or a percentage rent period at the start of your lease. These concessions can help you get a new business started.

☑ Accept reasonable rent steps for a longer-term lease, but don't accept aggressive rent steps that are going to cause the rent to rise much faster than your sales.

☑ Don't agree to a CPI increase in the rent. Also get out of any other rent increases that are built into the lease.

7

OVERAGE RENT

✦

It Sounds Bad, But You Will Want To Pay It

Most novice business owners first hear the words "percentage rent" or "overage rent" with fear and suspicion. Nearly all shopping center leases provide for the tenant to pay a percentage of its sales as additional or overage rent, and you must thoroughly understand how the overage rent is calculated.

OVERAGE RENT VS. PERCENTAGE RENT

The terms "overage rent" and "percentage rent" are used interchangeably. Most shopping center leases use the term "Percentage Rent" for both of the following situations. Both terms refer to a rent computed as a percentage of sales. But most in the shopping center industry make the following distinctions:

Overage Rent: The tenant pays an additional amount of rent, in addition to a fixed monthly rent, in addition to the minimum rent that was paid. The fixed monthly rent is referred to as "base rent" or "minimum rent."

Percentage Rent: The tenant pays only a percentage of sales as rent and does not pay a fixed monthly rent. The percentage rent is paid in arrears, after the sales are made.

OVERAGE RENT

Almost all shopping center leases contain an Overage Rent clause (although it might be called percentage rent in the lease). The tenant pays a percentage of the gross sales made from the premises as an additional rent, over and above the fixed rent. There are two methods typically used to determine the amount of the over-age rent. Both methods mathematically arrive at the same number if a *natural breakpoint* is used.

There are two methods typically found in leases that define how the Overage Rent will be computed:

Breakpoint Method: The tenant pays ___% of gross sales on all sales which exceed the sales breakpoint of $_____.

Deduct Base Rent Method: The tenant pays ___% of gross sales after deducting the minimum rent that was paid.

Both of the methods arrive at the same Overage Rent number, but are just computed differently. You should understand how the Overage Rent is computed in its lease.

SALES BREAKPOINT METHOD OF DETERMINING OVERAGE RENT

Sometimes the lease clause will require the tenant to pay overage rent as a percentage of sales over a certain sales breakpoint. The *sales breakpoint* is determined by *dividing the base rent by the percentage rate.* The math formula is simple algebra, solving for the unknown:

Sales Breakpoint: At what point does 6% of sales equal the base rent?

6% x ($ sales breakpoint) = ($ Base Rent)

($ Sales Breakpoint) = ($ Base Rent) / 6%

Example: Use the following example to see how a sales breakpoint is determined: Say the tenant agrees to pay overage rent of six percent (6%) of gross sales with a natural breakpoint. The tenant occupies 1,000 square feet with a base rent of $20 per square foot. The annual rent is $20,000.

You want to know at what point the base rent equals the percentage of gross sales (on an annual basis), which is the point over which the tenant pays the additional rent.

Formula:	6% x ($ sales breakpoint) = ($ base rent)
Example:	6% x ($ sales breakpoint) = $20,000
Convert percent to decimal:	0.06 x ($ sales breakpoint) = $20,000
Divide both sides:	($ sales breakpoint) = $20,000 / .06
Answer:	Sales Breakpoint = $333,333.33

The tenant would pay 6% of all sales over the gross sales amount of $333,333 per year. If the tenant's sales were, say, $350,000, the tenant would pay 6% of $16,667, or $1,000 in overage rent at the end of the year.

The tenant paid a total of $21,000 in rent—the $20,000 base rent plus the $1,000 overage rent. $21,000 is 6% of the gross sales of $350,000. No matter how much the gross sales are, as long as the sales exceed the breakpoint, the tenant will pay 6% in total annual rent. The base rent of $20,000 is paid up front, and the balance of the rent is paid as Overage Rent, after the sales are recorded.

"DEDUCT THE BASE RENT" METHOD OF DETERMINING OVERAGE RENT

Sometimes the shopping center lease clause will require the tenant to pay a percentage of sales of all gross sales, after deducting the base rent which was paid. This arrives at the same amount as the sales breakpoint method; it's just a different way of stating it.

The formula is simply: ___% of gross sales - ($ Base Rent) = Overage Rent.

Using the same numbers in the above example:

Example:	6% of $350,000 - $20,000 = Overage Rent
	$21,000 - $20,000 = Overage Rent
	$1,000 = Overage Rent

Usually the tenant and the landlord want to know the sales breakpoint, so even if the language in the lease uses the 'deduct the base rent' formula, the tenant and landlord will usually compute the sales breakpoint so they know at what level of sales the tenant must pay the additional rent.

DOES THE LEASE ALWAYS HAVE AN OVERAGE RENT CLAUSE?

Nearly all shopping center leases have an overage rent clause. The shopping center industry and shopping center leases are structured that way so the developer who built the shopping center receives the benefits of the higher rent if the shopping center is successful. Since most retail tenants are on long-term leases extending over many years, it is a way for the rent on the project to keep up with inflation.

DETERMINATION OF GROSS SALES

Typically, the tenant is required to compute overage rent on gross sales, which are the sales arising from the use of the premises, less sales taxes and other deductions. You will want to look closely at the list of allowable deductions and make sure the list is complete for your business.

Most landlords will allow the tenant to add some deductions to the lease clause, but the pre-written lease won't have these clauses. For example, most landlords will allow tenants to deduct sales to its employees, since these sales are usually made at a deep discount. Sales from employee break room vending machines, and other miscellaneous types of sales can also usually be deducted. You should make sure the list of exclusions for your business includes all potential income sources that you don't want to pay overage rent on.

An example of the importance of getting these deductions into the lease occurred recently with a local business owner. He had the foresight to make some changes to the lease document, adding language to be able to terminate the lease if gross sales ever fell below $500,000, and excluding sales to employees from "gross sales". After enjoying years of success in the shopping center, the store and the shopping center fell on difficult times, and sales plunged. His sales were just over $500,000, not low enough to allow him to cancel the lease. But when applying the deduction for employee sales, his gross sales came in below the threshold, and he was able to successfully negotiate out of the lease, saving thousands of dollars and eliminating a problem that might have brought his entire business down.

Add exclusions to your lease to exclude certain income from "gross sales".

SALES REPORTING

Most shopping center leases require the tenant to report its gross sales monthly, usually by the 15th or 20th of the following month. The sales reports are used to track the vitality and health of the overall shopping center, as well as to determine a tenant's overage rent. Some managers distribute reports to the tenants regularly to show how the center is performing, and how their store is performing in relation to others in the shopping center. These reports are valuable tools for the store manager. If your shopping center doesn't distribute a sales ranking report, you should occasionally meet with the shopping center manager and discuss how your sales compare to other stores in the center, and in the area.

Most leases also require the tenant to submit an annual sales report at the end of the year. Since many sales reports that are filed monthly are unedited estimates, the annual report is necessary to file a final, audited statement of sales.

MONTHLY OR ANNUAL OVERAGE RENT PAYMENTS

Overage Rent is almost always calculated on an *annual* basis. Usually, a *calendar year* basis is used, although some large chain tenants prefer to use their fiscal year basis. Sales are reported monthly during the year, and then at the end of the year, a final year-end sales statement is required from the tenant, and the Overage Rent is calculated against the year-end total.

Some shopping center leases require the tenant to pay Overage Rent*monthly*. This monthly payment is regarded as an estimate or an advance payment towards the total overage rent payment that is due at the end of the year. This is done by computing a *monthly sales breakpoint* and requiring the tenant to make an overage rent payment for sales that exceeded the *monthly* breakpoint.

If possible, you should get out of this monthly payment requirement. First, even for new retail businesses, it is possible to have a big sales month during the year where the monthly sales exceed that month's pro-rated breakpoint, requiring the tenant to make an overage rent payment. However, when averaged together with the other months, the total annual sales would not have exceeded the annual breakpoint. This is especially true if the retailer's peak sales season falls mid-year.

Any overage rent payments made during the year sit in the landlord's bank until next February when the year-end reports are completed and reconciled.

Secondly, when your retail business starts to mature and sales improve, it is highly likely that the year will come when you will exceed the sales breakpoint every month. If you have to pay the overage rent monthly, you don't get the benefits of keeping the extra cash on hand until later in the year.

If possible, try to get the landlord to agree to an *annual* overage rent payment, due about 60 days after the end of the year. This gives the business owner time to reconcile his accounts, make an accurate statement of sales, and make the overage rent payment.

If the landlord won't agree to an annual overage rent settlement and payment, the better alternative, and the way most tenants prefer it, is to start making overage rent payments monthly, but *after the month in which the sales breakpoint is exceeded.* In many cases the first time the sales breakpoint is exceeded is not until December, so it really acts as an annual requirement anyway. As your business matures and sales increase, the sales breakpoint might be exceeded earlier in the year, but still late enough that you are able to retain your funds in your bank or business until the end of the year. With a monthly requirement, you are paying the overage rent each month starting in January.

Make sure your lease says that you will pay Overage Rent after the sales breakpoint is reached. Do not make monthly Overage Rent payments.

NEGOTIATING THE PERCENTAGE RATE

Nearly all shopping center leases require the tenant to pay Overage Rent, but the actual percentage rate is negotiable. You usually end up paying more than most national tenants simply because they agree to the percentage rate that the leasing agent asks for.

Generally, the percentage rate varies from 5% to 8%. For a typical retail store, the leasing agent will ask for 7% or 8% but will almost always settle for 6%.

Rates vary on the type of merchandise being sold. Jewelry stores, for example, sell a higher-ticket item and can usually get the rate down to 5%. Food court restaurants, on the other hand, usually pay a higher rate of 7% or 8% because of the high margins in food sales. Computers and electronics generally have much thinner margin, and a lower rate.

Rates also vary on the type of tenant. National apparel chain stores will pay 5%, and sometimes 6%. Department stores and other large retailers might pay only 1.5% to 3%.

The best source to use to find average rates is the bi-annual publication by the Urban Land Institute, *Dollars and Cents of Shopping Centers.* The ULI compiles results from all types of shopping centers and give averages for rental rates. The book is usually available in University libraries, or the leasing agent or property manager may let you look at a copy.

However, the best negotiating tool to support your request for a lower percentage rate on the Overage Rent is your business plan and the margin on the types of products you will be selling. You need to look carefully at your projected financial statement to make sure you can afford to pay 8% of sales in rent if your average margin is only 35%.

Don't look casually at the Overage Rent rate and just agree to a higher rate than you should. Don't look at the sales breakpoint and think to yourself that you'll never hit that point anyway. When your store takes off two or three years later, the store sales have easily exceeded the sales breakpoint. Even though sales are high, you are not making a lot of profit. It's almost impossible at that point to reduce the percentage rate—negotiate it before signing the lease.

Be cautious about agreeing to an Overage Rent percentage rate higher than 6%. The rate is negotiable, and the lower the rate, the lower the total rent you may pay later on.

RELATIONSHIP BETWEEN BASE RENT AND THE SALES BREAKPOINT

Another common mistake you might make when negotiating a lease is failing to consider the relationship between the Overage Rent sales breakpoint and the Base Rent. Many people will argue at length to get a lower Base Rent, because that is what they focus on—the monthly rent payment they have to make. They want to get their monthly payment as low as possible. But those who know how Overage

Rent works know that the lower the Base Rent, the lower the sales breakpoint for Overage Rent.

It is common for an owner to start a lease with a lower Base Rent. However, if the store is successful and hits even an average level of sales, the owner is into Overage Rent as soon as he meets his sales projections. But in the beginning of a new lease, the owner doesn't always stop to consider his total rent bill—the owner is so focused on the lower monthly rent, fails to look at the rest of the formula, and fails to plan for the Overage Rent payments that are coming due.

Example: Assume a store with 1,000 square feet, Overage Rent of 6%, and Base Rent of $20,000 per year ($20 PSF). In the above example, we determined the sales breakpoint would be $333,333 ($20,000 / .06). If the owner's store achieves the average level of sales of $300,000 ($300 PSF), no Overage Rent is due. But if the owner successfully negotiates a lower base rent, say, in the first year or two of the lease term, what happens to the sales breakpoint? It also goes down.

If the rent were reduced to $15 per square foot, or $15,000 per year, the breakpoint would go down commensurately. The formula to find the sales breakpoint is *the base rent divided by the percentage rate*, so the revised breakpoint is $250,000 ($15,000 / .06). If the store hits the average sales of $300,000 in the first year or two, the owner will pay 6% of $50,000 in Overage Rent, or another $3,000, for a total effective rent of $18,000.

The $18,000 is less than the $20,000 Base Rent, and so the owner negotiated a good deal, but many owners fall into the trap of forgetting about the Overage Rent and concentrating solely on the Base Rent. When the invoice for $3,000 comes, they are not prepared for it. Remember that the Base Rent is often called the Minimum Rent, and that the lease also requires Overage Rent. Both together are the total rent that the tenant pays.

On the other hand, when the Base Rent increases, the sales breakpoint also increases. When it comes time for an increase in the Base Rent, either for a step increase in the lease, or for a lease extension, recalculate the sales breakpoint to determine the total effective rent you will be paying.

Plan for the total rent you will pay, not just the base rent.

RELATIONSHIP BETWEEN PERCENTAGE RATE AND THE SALES BREAKPOINT

The sales breakpoint also changes when the percentage rate changes. When the rate is lowered, the sales breakpoint is higher. When the percentage rate is higher, the breakpoint is lower.

Sometimes a tenant will agree to a higher percentage rate for the Overage Rent rate, and not understand that the breakpoint is going to be lower.

Example: At the $18,000 annual base rent, and an Overage Rent percentage of 6%, the breakpoint is $300,000. If the Overage Rent percentage is increased to 7%, the breakpoint is $257,143. If the Overage Rent percentage is decreased to 5%, the breakpoint is $360,000.

A 1-point change in the Overage Rent rate makes a big difference in the total amount of effective rent you will pay; so don't overlook this in your quest to get a lower monthly base rent. When negotiating, don't agree to a higher percentage rent rate in exchange for a lower base rent. It will come back to bite you.

UNNATURAL SALES BREAKPOINTS

The examples we have been using are referred to as a *natural breakpoint*. The sales breakpoint is the point at which the Base Rent equals the percentage of sales. Example: $18,000 rent and 6% Overage Rent rate: the *natural* breakpoint is $300,000, the point where 6% equals $18,000.

There are occasionally leases that have an *unnatural breakpoint*. The sales breakpoint is simply determined by agreement between the parties. Most often, this is done for larger retailers, but it is not unusual to see such an agreement for a small tenant.

Using the above example, you might say to the leasing agent, "I will pay your $18,000 Base Rent, but reduce my Overage Rent rate to 4% over the $300,000 sales breakpoint." In effect, you are paying 6% rent on sales of $300,000, but 4% on sales over $300,000.

You could also do the reverse—agree to pay a higher percentage rate if the sales go above a breakpoint. Once your fixed costs are paid for, you could agree to a higher percentage on those sales that come in at a higher level.

An unnaturally high breakpoint agreement is usually made when the Base Rent is high. On the other hand, an unnaturally low breakpoint agreement might be made if the Base Rent was extremely low.

In most cases, however, the natural breakpoint is used.

OVERAGE RENT IN PARTIAL YEARS

The effect of Overage Rent in a partial year trips up a lot of tenants and causes them to pay more rent in the first year of the lease term. Say a retail business opens in mid-October, which is typical—opening just before the busy Holiday Season. The business owner might owe percentage rent for the first partial lease year, which would be from opening through December 31st. Because sales are high in December, and the business wasn't open the slower months of the year, the business owner will pay percentage rent if a standard pro-rated calculation is done.

Example: The lease for a retail business calls for Base Rent of $24,000 per year and Overage Rent of 6% over $400,000 (natural breakpoint). The business opens on November 1st and thus paid $4,000 in Base Rent for the two months. Sales for the first two months are very brisk—$80,000 from opening through the end of the year. Now calculate if any overage rent is due. To figure the pro-rated breakpoint, use the same formula as computing an annual breakpoint:

Base Rent divided by Percentage Rate = Overage Rent Breakpoint

$4,000 / .06 = $66,667

$80,000 sales - $66,667 breakpoint = $13,333 subject to Overage Rent

$13,333 * .06 = <u>$800 Overage Rent</u>

If the same store was open for a full year, and all of the months were averaged together, the store would probably *owe no Overage Rent.* But because only the two highest-sales months of the year are pro-rated, the business owner exceeded the pro-rated breakpoint and now owes another $800 in Overage Rent. Ouch!

To avoid this, if you are planning to open your retail store at the end of the year make sure you put some protection into the lease to avoid having to pay percentage rent the first partial year. Just ask for an agreement that no Overage Rent is due for the first partial year. It is likely the landlord will agree, but if the landlord balks, you can use an artificially high breakpoint for the first partial year that lowers your exposure.

If you are opening your store early in the year and have the benefit of averaging several more months of sales, this is probably not an issue. But if you are opening at the end of the year, watch out for this extra surprise payment you will have to make.

OVERAGE RENT CHECKLIST:

When negotiating a shopping center lease, remember these points:

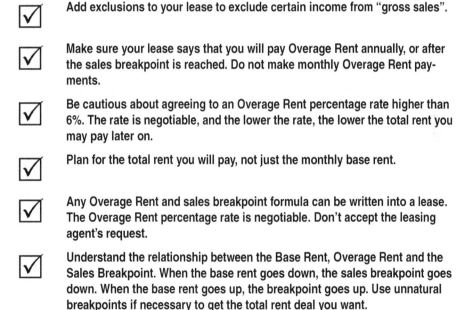

☑ Add exclusions to your lease to exclude certain income from "gross sales".

☑ Make sure your lease says that you will pay Overage Rent annually, or after the sales breakpoint is reached. Do not make monthly Overage Rent payments.

☑ Be cautious about agreeing to an Overage Rent percentage rate higher than 6%. The rate is negotiable, and the lower the rate, the lower the total rent you may pay later on.

☑ Plan for the total rent you will pay, not just the monthly base rent.

☑ Any Overage Rent and sales breakpoint formula can be written into a lease. The Overage Rent percentage rate is negotiable. Don't accept the leasing agent's request.

☑ Understand the relationship between the Base Rent, Overage Rent and the Sales Breakpoint. When the base rent goes down, the sales breakpoint goes down. When the base rent goes up, the breakpoint goes up. Use unnatural breakpoints if necessary to get the total rent deal you want.

☑ Watch out for the partial year pro-rated breakpoint if you are opening late in the calendar year.

8

PERCENTAGE RENT

✦

Not To Be Confused With Overage Rent

Although most leases use the term "Percentage Rent" to refer to both Overage Rent and straight percentage rent, the term *Percentage Rent* has come to mean a lease agreement where the tenant pays a straight percentage of the sales in arrears, in lieu of a fixed rent payment in advance.

WHEN PERCENTAGE RENT IS USED

A Percentage Rent agreement is typically used in these types of instances:

As a start-up rent formula

On a temporary agreement

On a rent adjustment for a failing tenant

As an alternative rent when co-occupancy or other conditions in the lease are not met

Typically a percentage rent agreement is used only on a **short-term basis,** or at least that is how landlords would like to see it.

Temporary Tenants: Some *temporary tenant* agreements will use a percentage rent only. If the shopping center is struggling to remain viable and has a large number of vacant spaces, the management may allow start-up tenants to come in on a short-term basis and "see what they can do." A straight percentage rent is one way to start such tenants out, since it is unlikely that the tenant will be able to pay any Base Rent to start with. Allowing the tenant to pay a percentage of its sales after the sales have been generated gives the tenant a running chance to get his/her business started.

Start-Up Businesses: Occasionally, a successful shopping center with few vacancies will agree to a straight percentage rent deal. If a new tenant has a start up business that looks interesting and promising, offering the tenant a straight percentage rent on a short term, start-up basis might be beneficial. Later, if the tenant succeeds, a standard longer-term lease can be written.

Rent Relief: Another instance where a straight percentage rent is often used is when a tenant on a longer-term lease is failing and needs a break on the rent for a short time to turn the business around. Sometimes the shopping center management will agree it is better to work with a tenant who is struggling rather than lose the tenant entirely. Typically, a 6-month period is offered where the tenant can pay a percentage of sales in arrears in lieu of the Base Rent and other charges in the lease.

Alternative Rent: Often, tenants who successfully negotiate co-occupancy requirements[1] or other checkpoints into their lease will negotiate an alternative percentage rent if the co-occupancy or other requirement is not met.

PERCENTAGE RENT: GROSS OR NET

The term "rent" has different interpretations. For some, the term "rent" refers to just the Base Rent in the lease, not including the CAM, Real Estate Taxes, and other payments the tenant has to pay. For others, the term "rent" refers to all of the payments the tenant has to pay.

Make sure it is spelled out in the agreement, and make sure you understand what the agreement says. Too often, tenants carelessly or unknowingly agree to pay a 10% straight percentage rent, and then find out they have to pay the additional charges also, which means they might be paying 15% to 20% in total, when they thought they were only going to pay 10% in total.

Sometimes the Base Rent is referred to as the *Net Base Rent*, because it is net of the other charges in the lease. The term *Gross Rent* would refer to the entire

---

1. See Chapter on "Special Lease Provisions" for explanation of Co-Occupancy and other provisions.

amount the tenant has to pay. Sometimes you hear the term *All-In*, which is another way of saying all of the charges the tenant has to pay.

Make sure you know what is included in the "Percentage Rent". Is it net or gross?

PERCENTAGE RENT RATE

Typically, a straight percentage rent rate will be higher than an Overage Rent rate. With Overage Rent, the tenant pays a Base Rent monthly, and then an additional Overage Rent payment as a percent of sales over a certain breakpoint. But with straight Percentage Rent, the rate is usually higher. There is no upfront payment, or base rent. This is a good deal for the tenant but a higher risk for the landlord.

A standard 10% to 12% in lieu of all charges is pretty typical for a straight percentage rent deal. 15% might still be reasonable for some products, especially in high traffic locations where sales are expected to be high.

If the tenant is going to be required to pay the additional charges such as CAM, Real Estate Taxes, and Marketing Fund, then the net percentage rate should be lower to keep the total in line with the total occupancy cost the tenant is paying. Add up the total of the other charges and determine what percent of sales the payments are likely to represent, and then set the percentage rent rate so the sum of all the payments meets the 10% to 12% formula.

For example, if a tenant is doing about $25,000 per month in sales and its CAM, taxes, and other payments are about $1,500 per month; the other payments represent about 6% of the total monthly sales ($1500 / $25,000). A percentage-in-lieu-of-base-rent-only deal might be about 5%, for a total payment of 11%.

On the other hand, if the tenant in the same example were offered a gross percentage deal, which would be in lieu of all the charges in the lease, the tenant would agree to pay 10% or 11% *all-in*.

Set the percentage rent rate at a level that makes sense for your business.

GOING ON/OFF PERCENTAGE RENT

Since a straight Percentage Rent is usually for a short time period, there is a potential pitfall that often trips up tenants when going on and off the percentage rent period. *Percentage rent is paid in arrears—Base Rent is paid in advance.*

This can be a problem in situations when switching from Percentage Rent to Base Rent. For example: say you negotiates a 3-year lease where you pay Percentage Rent only during the first 6 months of the lease term, and then pay Base Rent every month thereafter. The Percentage Rent will be due on the 15th of the following month; and the Base Rent will be due on the first of the month. In this situation, you would not pay any rent at all for the first 45 days of occupancy, but in the seventh month, you would have to pay two months rent: the Base Rent in advance on the first of the month, and percentage rent for the sixth month on the 15th.

Although the Percentage Rent is helpful in the first few months to give the business owner a chance to get the business going before committing to high rent payments, you can run into a problem when switching to the Base Rent. Be prepared for this.

PERCENTAGE RENT CHECKLIST

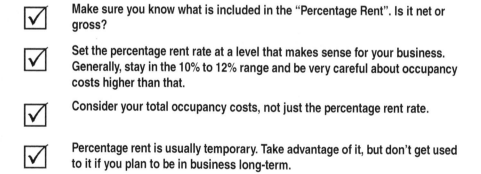

☑ Make sure you know what is included in the "Percentage Rent". Is it net or gross?

☑ Set the percentage rent rate at a level that makes sense for your business. Generally, stay in the 10% to 12% range and be very careful about occupancy costs higher than that.

☑ Consider your total occupancy costs, not just the percentage rent rate.

☑ Percentage rent is usually temporary. Take advantage of it, but don't get used to it if you plan to be in business long-term.

9

COMMON AREA
MAINTENANCE

❖

Sometimes CAM is More than Rent

Typically, shopping center leases provide that the tenants pay for all of the costs of maintaining and operating the common areas of the shopping center. The shopping center lease is a "triple net" lease, which means that the "rent" the landlord receives is net of the expenses of operating the shopping center. This is generally different than residential and other types of leased property where the landlord has to pay the expenses out of the rent received. The Common Area Maintenance (CAM) costs can be a large expense for tenants of large, enclosed malls and other shopping centers with high maintenance costs. For smaller shopping centers with no enclosed area, the CAM costs can be much less expensive.

WHAT COSTS ARE INCLUDED IN CAM?

The lease will have a page or two describing in some detail what expenses are included as CAM costs. Generally, all of the expenses to maintain the shopping center, such as cleaning, sweeping, lighting, landscaping, etc. are included in CAM, and these items are pretty straightforward. But the tenant should be wary when an item that is vague and nonspecific, such as "repainting", is listed in CAM costs. Repainting what? Are the tenants going to pay for the cost of repainting the exterior of the department stores? It is important that all CAM items be defined as applying specifically to the common areas.

The CAM provision must be read carefully. In one developer's lease, there was an article 15 that spelled out what maintenance the tenant was responsible for, and what maintenance the landlord was responsible for. Article 15 required the tenant to maintain the interior of its own store and so on, while the landlord was responsible for maintaining the roof, the exterior walls, the main utility lines and other structural portions of the premises. Okay, this clause sounds reasonable. But later in the lease in the article that described what was included in CAM the following was listed among the items included in CAM: "and all expenses per Article 15 of this lease". So even though the maintenance clause stated that it was the landlord's responsibility to maintain the roof and other structural items, the costs of that maintenance were included in another section of the lease as a CAM expense. Only a few careful readers of the CAM clause ever caught this. Mostly they were the national tenants who had attorneys on staff with the time and experience to read every item included in the definition of CAM items. In every case where the tenant brought up an objection to this clause, the reference to Article 15 costs was deleted from CAM, thus saving the tenant exposure to paying for a share of some very expensive costs.

There are two factors that drive up the costs of CAM expenses: *the pro-rata share* the tenant pays, and the *actual cost of the CAM expenses*. Even if the actual costs of CAM expenses are decreasing, the tenant might be hit with stiff CAM increases if the occupancy of the shopping center is falling.

THE PRO-RATA SHARE

The shopping center lease goes into lengthy detail about how the tenant's share of CAM costs is calculated. Typically, the tenant pays for a pro-rata share of the total CAM expenses based on the size of the tenant's leased space. For example, if a tenant leased 1,000 square feet in a 10,000 square foot shopping center, the tenant's share would be 10%. The landlord would keep track of the entire CAM expenses incurred and charge the tenant 10% of the total. In smaller centers, it seems pretty simple and straightforward, but in larger shopping centers, it's not that simple and the tenant needs to be careful.

To analyze the pro-rata share a tenant pays; think of the tenant's share as a fraction. The numerator (the top part of the fraction) is the size of the tenant's space. The denominator (the bottom part of the fraction) is the total size of the shopping center. The numerator (tenant's space size) is simple—it's fixed in the lease. But the denominator is subject to definition, interpretation and negotiation. In a larger center, the large anchor tenants are generally excluded from the denominator in calculating the tenant's pro-rata share of CAM. Why? Because the large stores don't usually pay a full share of CAM. So the denominator in an 800,000 sf mall with three anchors accounting for 450,000 sf would be 350,000 sf. A tenant with 1,000 square feet of space pays a much bigger pro-rata share with a smaller denominator. The thing to watch out for, then, is how the lease defines an anchor tenant. Some leases refer to a lease plan or name the department stores by name or location, but other leases will say that "any tenant over 25,000 sf" is not included in the denominator.

In negotiating, it is unlikely that a small tenant can demand that the anchor stores be included in the pro-rata calculation, or otherwise change the way the landlord calculates the pro-rata share, but the tenant can make sure there is a clear definition of its pro-rata share in the lease to avoid confusion later.

There is another part of the pro-rata calculation that directly affects the tenant's CAM costs, and that is the difference between *leaseable* and *open and occupied* square footage. Some leases state that the denominator in the tenant's pro-rata share calculation will be the total leaseable square footage of the shopping center (not including the major tenants). In this case, in the above example, the denominator would be the full 350,000 sf. However, many shopping center leases state define the denominator to be the total square footage of the shopping center that is open and occupied by other tenants. This clause really opens up the tenant's exposure to a higher pro-rata calculation. If the center falls on hard times, or if it is just getting started, it is not uncommon to see occupancy as low as 70% (or less). 70% of the total 350,000 sf is 255,000 sf, so the tenant ends up paying a much higher pro-rata share.

It is an obvious benefit for the landlord to divide all the CAM expenses among the tenants in the center, even if only half the center is leased. If there was 30% occupancy and the CAM costs were calculated on total leaseable square footage, the landlord would not be able to recover the CAM expenses from the vacant space. Since many of the expenses aren't necessarily related to occupancy, lighting for example, the tenants in a high-vacancy shopping center pay a higher pro-rata share if their lease provides for the denominator of open and occupied space.

There are some ways to negotiate some protection for the tenant into the lease. Many national tenants simply won't agree to an *open and occupied* definition in the pro-rata share calculation, and will change the language in the lease to provide for a total *leaseable* denominator. It is also not uncommon for tenants to negotiate an occupancy cap into the lease that provides that the occupancy used in the calculation can not be less than, say, 90% or 85%. Another way is to simply set forth a fixed pro-rata share for the tenant in the lease, such as 0.15%. This might work in a smaller shopping center or in a short-term lease, but in a larger center where there is room for expansion, the tenant would lose the benefit of any *increased* square footage that could have been added to the denominator to decrease the tenant's pro-rata share.

HOW IS OCCUPANCY DETERMINED?

The denominator in a tenant's pro-rata share is affected by the total occupancy of the center, but at what point in time is the occupancy determined? Most landlords will only compute the tenant's actual pro-rata share once a year; it would be too time consuming to do it more often. So at what point in the year is the share calculated? If the landlord bases the occupancy on January 1st, and some large tenants opened mid-year, the tenant is not going to receive the benefit of the higher occupancy in the denominator when the pro-rata share is calculated. On the other hand, if the landlord uses the occupancy as of the last day of the year to calculate the share, and a large tenant closed on December 29th, the tenant's share would not receive credit for almost a whole year of shared occupancy.

The best way is probably to average the occupancy levels monthly. But many leases provide for a quarterly average, or some other calculation, and some leases are silent on this point. Make sure the method of determining the occupancy is spelled out in the lease, and that it is reasonable.

ANCHOR STORE CAM CONTRIBUTIONS

As explained above, the typical shopping center lease does not count the anchor stores leased area as part of the denominator in determining a tenant's pro-rata share. This is because a large store usually won't agree to pay a full pro-rata share of the CAM expenses.

However, the large anchor tenants usually pay *something* towards CAM, even if it's a low percentage of the total. Make sure the lease clearly spells out how the *contributions* from the anchor tenants are handled. Typically, the lease will provide that any contribution made towards CAM expenses will be deducted from the total CAM expenses before allocating the remainder to the rest of the tenants.

But some leases are silent on this—leaving it up to the whim of the landlord if the anchor contributions are to be credited to the other tenants.

CAM contributions from temporary tenants must also be spelled out in the lease. Most shopping centers will lease cart space and kiosk spaces in the common areas of the shopping center. If these cart and kiosk tenants are going to make payments for CAM expenses, make sure the lease defines how these payments are handled. If the cart and kiosk leaseable area is not included in the denominator, then any contributions that these tenants make should be deducted from the total CAM expenses before calculating the tenant's share of expenses.

ACTUAL CAM EXPENSE INCREASES

The other factors that can drive up a tenant's CAM expenses, of course, are the actual costs to maintain the shopping center. These expenses almost always increase over time as costs increase. Since the tenants have no control over the maintenance of the common area, heavy CAM increases trouble many tenants. Some are suspicious of landlords who pass through all of the expenses to the tenants, and then charge a supervision fee that is a percentage of the total CAM costs.

It is not unreasonable for tenants to negotiate for some protection in the lease against escalating CAM expenses. Typically, this is accomplished with a cap on the amount of increases in the total CAM expenses in any one year, say, putting a 5% per year limit. These clauses can be confusing and must be carefully worded. For example, if the total CAM expenses go up 2% one year and then 6% the next year, does a 5% cap mean a 5% average, in which case the tenant would have to pay the full 6% increase in year 2? Or does a 5% cap mean just a simple "not to exceed 5% in one year"?

To make it more confusing, when tenants are negotiating for a cap on CAM increases, some landlords might want to exclude certain items from the cap. For example, snow removal costs are directly determined by how much it snows, and a sharp landlord probably wouldn't want to include those costs in a cap, but might agree to cap controllable expenses.

CUMULATIVE AND NON-CUMULATIVE INCREASE CAPS

The difference between cumulative and non-cumulative increases is important. A non-cumulative increase means that the costs won't increase more than 5% for that one year compared to the prior year. A cumulative increase means the cap grows by 5% per year regardless of the actual increases each year.

Example of a *non-cumulative* 5% increase cap: Say the costs for the CAM billing started at $8.00 per square foot and the actual expenses increased 2% the first year, 3% the second year, and 8% the third year. Over a three-year period, the costs would increase to $8.16, $8.40, and $9.07 PSF in the respective years. If the tenant had a lease provision limiting the annual increase to 5% on a non-cumulative basis, the increase in the third year would be limited to the 5% cap and the tenant would save the difference—$8.82 PSF compared to the $9.07 PSF.

Example of a *cumulative* 5% increase cap: Say the costs for a billing item started at $8.00 per square foot at the commencement of the lease, and increased at the same as the above example—2%, 3% and 8%. Over a three-year period, the costs would increase to $8.16, $8.40, and $9.07 PSF in the respective years. The 5% cumulative cap would grow each year by 5% so starting at $8.00; the cap for the 3 years would be $8.40, $8.82, and $9.26. So even though there was an 8% increase in the third year, the cost would still be under the *cumulative 5% cap* so the tenant would have to pay the increase.

Over a long-term lease, the cumulative cap can grow much faster than the actual increase in expenses, resulting in no protection for the tenant from big increases in later years of the lease.

If the tenant requests a 5% cap on expenses, and if the landlord agrees, the landlord will try to make it a *cumulative cap* because the landlord understands the difference. If you don't understand the difference, you will not get the protection you are seeking for large increases in any one year.

CAPITAL EXPENSE VS. CAM EXPENSE

Remodel costs and other capital expenses almost always cause arguments between landlords and tenants over what can be included in CAM expenses. When a shopping center is being remodeled, the landlord will try to recover as much of the costs of the remodel from the tenants as possible. With no protection in the lease, a tenant can be faced with huge CAM expenses during the remodel of a shopping center.

For example, what is meant when the CAM definition in the lease provides for "replacement of floor tile"? The tenant would argue that the replacement of an occasional broken tile subject to normal routine maintenance is all that should be included in CAM, but the landlord looking to recover costs of a remodel would argue that replacement means total replacement as well as one or two at a time.

Tenants can protect themselves by making sure that the lease defines clearly how the costs of capital improvements are going to be handled in CAM costs, if at all. Some leases might provide for certain capital expenses, which exceed an amount of, say $10,000, and be amortized over a period of useful life. That way the tenant is not charged for a large capital item in any one year, but the cost is spread out over several years. No tenant would want the costs of a shopping center remodel to be included in CAM costs, and only a careful reading of the lease and negotiating clarifications can accomplish this.

NEGOTIATE THE CAM CLAUSE IN THE LEASE

Local tenants never challenge the CAM clause in the shopping center lease, simply because they don't understand CAM and how it is calculated. They just accept the pre-written lease language and hope for the best.

National tenants, on the other hand, seldom accept the standard CAM clause pre-written into the lease. They insert paragraphs and even pages of clarifications, exclusions, caps, and explanations.

As a result, you end up paying a higher share and more expensive CAM costs. Negotiate the CAM clause. Make sure the CAM expenses are clearly defined, get a cap on CAM increases, get a smaller denominator, and get a cap on occupancy levels.

How do you do this? Just ask for it. Make it part of the deal up-front, with the leasing agent. Get it into a letter. The leasing agent will be eager to close the lease deal, and he will agree to reasonable changes to the CAM language. If you fail to discuss these items with the leasing agent, and wait until you have agreed to a rent deal, it can be more difficult to get changes into the lease. By then, you are dealing with attorneys and they are not as quick to agree to changes (although they will make changes, but it takes longer).

The CAM clause is important. It is a high cost of renting space in a shopping center, and deserves as much negotiation as the base rent and overage rent. Don't hesitate to negotiate some protection into your lease against high CAM fees.

CAM CHECKLIST

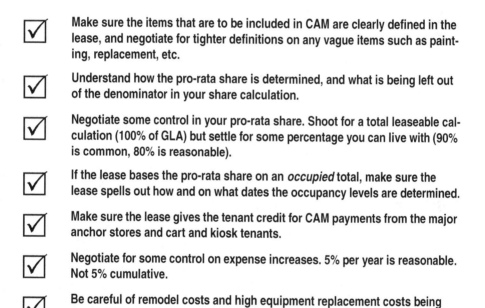

☑ Make sure the items that are to be included in CAM are clearly defined in the lease, and negotiate for tighter definitions on any vague items such as painting, replacement, etc.

☑ Understand how the pro-rata share is determined, and what is being left out of the denominator in your share calculation.

☑ Negotiate some control in your pro-rata share. Shoot for a total leaseable calculation (100% of GLA) but settle for some percentage you can live with (90% is common, 80% is reasonable).

☑ If the lease bases the pro-rata share on an *occupied* total, make sure the lease spells out how and on what dates the occupancy levels are determined.

☑ Make sure the lease gives the tenant credit for CAM payments from the major anchor stores and cart and kiosk tenants.

☑ Negotiate for some control on expense increases. 5% per year is reasonable. Not 5% cumulative.

☑ Be careful of remodel costs and high equipment replacement costs being passed through by the landlord as CAM expenses. Make sure your lease either excludes these costs, or, at the least, offers some amortization of the higher capital expenses.

10

REAL ESTATE TAXES

◆

Someone Has to Pay Them

Almost all shopping center leases require the tenants to pay for the cost of Real Estate Taxes assessed against the shopping center property. Typically, there are not separate tax parcels for each separate lease space in a shopping center, so the tax bill is pro-rated on a square footage basis among the tenants whose lease spaces are in a particular tax parcel.

PRO-RATA SHARE

Ordinarily, the shopping center lease provides for the tenant to pay a pro-rata share of the real estate tax expense, often referred to in shopping center accounting as "RET". The share is determined by using a fraction: dividing the square footage of the tenant's leased area (numerator) by the *total leasable area* of the shopping center in that tax parcel (denominator). There may be some leases that are written to determine the tenant's pro-rata share by using the *leased and occupied* square footage as the denominator of the fraction. If there is a lot of vacancy in the shopping center, the tenant will pay a higher percentage of the tax bill with a *leased and occupied* denominator. Try to get this changed in the lease negotiations to a share based on the *total leasable area*.

For smaller tenants in a shopping center, the taxes are estimated and paid monthly with the rent, similar to an escrow payment to a mortgage lender. The taxes are estimated at the beginning of each year, and a monthly estimate is determined for the tenant. When the tax bill arrives, the landlord pays it and then makes an accounting to the tenants, usually at the end of the calendar year. Any excess that the tenant paid is refunded, and any shortage is billed to the tenant.

Some taxing jurisdictions are on a calendar year—tax year basis, and some juris-dictions are on a fiscal year—tax year basis. If your lease provides for the taxes (and other expenses) to be reconciled on a calendar year basis, each calendar year will involve two tax years—the latter half of one year and the earlier half of the second tax year. This can result in a confusing allocation and settlement at the end of the year, so it's a good idea to go over the settlement statement and ask any questions as needed.

Many shopping center leases add an administrative fee of 15% to the Real Estate Tax bill before billing the taxes back to the tenants. Almost all chain stores can get this admin fee deleted from the Real Estate Taxes. You can likely get it deleted, too. It was formerly the custom among landlords not to charge an administrative fee on taxes and insurance, but that custom has changed in more recent leases.

Example: If a shopping center has 500,000 square feet of Gross Leasable Area (GLA) and a tenant has 2,000 SF of leased area, the tenant's share on a ***total leasable basis*** is 2,000/500,000, or 0.40%. If the Real Estate Taxes were $1 Million per year, the tenant's billing would by 0.40% of $1 Million, or $4,000 per year.

If the same tenant's lease in the same shopping center provided for a calculation based on *leased and occupied basis*, and the shopping center were only 70% leased, the tenant's share would be 2,000/350,000, or 0.57%. On the same tax bill, the tenant's billing would be $5,700 per year.

And if the 15% admin fee were included in the lease, the tenant would pay an additional $600 to $855 over and above the tax billing. Would you rather pay $4,000 or $6,555 for the same tax bill in the same shopping center? It's all in how you negotiate your lease, but you have to ask for it.

COMMON AREA REAL ESTATE TAXES

Since a portion of the tax parcel for a shopping center probably includes the common areas of the shopping center as well as the leased space, it is important to see how the landlord's lease handles the taxes for the common area.

In some leases, the taxes on the common areas are allocated using the same method as determining the allocation for a tenant space: take the total square footage of the common areas divided by the total square footage of the improvements in the tax bill. This allocation of the tax bill is then added to the Common Area Maintenance (CAM) expenses for the center. Usually the lease provides for the landlord to collect a 15% administrative and supervision surcharge on the CAM expenses. So, by taking an allocation of the real estate taxes and adding it to the CAM expenses, the landlord collects the 15% surcharge, even if the landlord doesn't collect the 15% admin fee on RET. Some tenants have successfully negotiated to have this surcharge waived for the tax payments in CAM. You should try to do the same—no 15% fee on Real Estate Taxes, either those taxes pro-rated on the tenant premises, or those taxes allocated to the common areas.

Another benefit to the landlord of allocating part of the tax expense to CAM is that the CAM expenses are usually pro-rated among the tenants by the *leased and occupied* square footage of the shopping center, not the *total leasable* square footage. The landlord is then able to bill back a higher percentage to the tenant through CAM.

The alternative way to handle the allocation of taxes to the common areas is not to allocate any tax expenses to the common areas, and just simply pro-rate the entire tax bill among the tenant leasable area, excluding the common areas. Each tenant would pay its pro-rata share of the taxes on the common areas anyway. It only benefits the landlord to add those tax expenses into CAM. Some major tenants have been successful in getting the lease revised so that tax is not included in CAM, and there is no admin fee.

Make sure your lease fairly allocates the Real Estate taxes—try to have the taxes allocated on a total leasable basis when possible, without an allocation to CAM. If you can't get out of the CAM allocation, make sure you have protection in your lease on the total CAM expenses.[1]

TAX REFUNDS AND PROTESTS

Occasionally, a shopping center will be successful in protesting a tax assessment and will get a tax refund for a tax year when the taxes have already been paid. Unless the lease provides for the landlord to rebate the refund back to the tenants, there may not be any requirement for the landlord to do so. Read your lease and make sure that any refunds are given back to the tenant on the same pro-rata method as the tax billing.

---

1.   See Chapter on Common Area Maintenance for description of various CAM clauses.

Frequently, a professional tax consultant is hired by the landlord to protest the taxes with the taxing jurisdiction. The fees for the tax consultant are generally included in the total RET billed back to tenants. This is probably fair, since the tenants benefit from the lower taxes.

TENANT IMPROVEMENT TAXES

Some taxing jurisdictions attempt to tax the tenant improvements (TI) within the leased premises of a shopping center property separately from the basic real estate. If your taxing jurisdiction does this, be very careful about how the lease treats these taxes. In most cases, if there is a separate tax bill on the tenant improvements, the lease will provide for the tenant to pay for the TI taxes. The basic taxes on the real estate land and shopping center structure will then be pro-rated among the tenants.

But what happens when a tenant moves out? The tenant has abandoned the tenant improvements and so the taxing jurisdiction must send the tax bill somewhere, so they send it to the landlord. Does the landlord pay for the taxes on those improvements out of its own pocket, or is that tax bill added with the other tax bills on the structure and common areas and billed back to the tenants in that parcel? If it is lumped in and billed back, the other tenants are paying taxes on the departed tenant's TI, plus they are paying their own taxes on their own TI.

Other jurisdictions ignore tenant improvements and don't try to assess each separate tenant in a shopping center for the individual TI—they just assess the entire shopping center based on total value.

Find out how the jurisdiction in your area treats the tenant improvements, and read the lease to make sure this is handled fairly. Otherwise, you could end up paying for your own tenant improvements, and a pro-rata share of other space improvements. If the taxing agency bills tenants separately for the value of TI, and the lease is silent on how the TI taxes are treated, add an addendum to the lease to require that taxes on TI are never to be added to the RET in the lease.

Although the RET billing is not as high as the CAM billing, you can still save thousands of dollars a year in tax billings. Don't forget to negotiate up front for these concessions—get them into the business letter.

RET CHECKLIST

☑ Get the RET pro-rated on the basis of the *total leasable area* of the shopping center, not the *open and occupied area*, which would increase your share of the tax bill.

☑ Delete the 15% administrative fee for RET.

☑ Try to avoid having a portion of the taxes allocated to CAM. Instead, try to have the total taxes allocated to the premises on a total leasable basis with no administration fee.

☑ Make sure the lease accounts for the proper handling of taxes on Tenant Improvements.

☑ Most landlords will not agree to a cap on tax increases, since they have no control over the increase.

11

INSURANCE

✦

Insurance Is an Important Requirement of Shopping Center Leases

In almost all shopping center leases, both the tenant and the landlord are required to carry certain types of insurance. There are two basic types of insurance, "property/casualty" and "liability." Typically, the landlord carries **property insurance** on the building structure and the tenant carries insurance on the tenant improvements and inventory in the tenant's premises. The landlord carries **liability insurance** on the common areas of the property, and the tenant carries liability insurance for the tenant's premises.

PROPERTY INSURANCE

In most shopping center leases, the landlord provides the property insurance for the shopping center to insure the structure against the perils of fire and other casualties. However, in most shopping center leases, the cost of the insurance is billed back to the tenants on a pro-rata basis.

In most cases, the landlord's property insurance only provides coverage to rebuild the shopping center structure in the event of a major casualty—it won't provide coverage to rebuild the tenants' stores, such as the ceilings, walls, furnishings and inventory inside the tenants' premises.

TENANT BILLINGS FOR PROPERTY INSURANCE

In some leases, the expenses of Property Insurance and Liability Insurance are handled differently. Property Insurance may be pro-rated and billed to the tenants separately, while liability insurance is included in CAM. In other leases, the expense of the two types of insurance is handled as a CAM item.

INS Billing

When the two types of insurance are handled differently, most "triple net" shopping center leases provide for the landlord to bill the cost of the property insurance (INS) back to the tenants on a square footage basis. There are two basic ways to do this: on a *leased and occupied* basis, or a *total leasable* basis. The tenant wants the insurance billing to be done on a *total leasable* basis, which means that the tenant's pro-rata share is calculated by the entire square footage of leasable space in the shopping center, or 100% of the Gross Leasable Area. A calculation based on a share of the *leased* area means that the tenant's share is calculated by only the square footage of the property that is leased. If there were a lot of vacancy, the tenant's share of the expense would be much higher.

Example: If a shopping center has 500,000 square feet of Gross Leasable Area (GLA) and a tenant has 2,000 SF of leased area, the tenant's share on a *total leasable basis* is 2,000/500,000, or 0.40%. If the insurance premium was $40,000 per year, the tenant's billing would by 0.40% of $40,000, or $160 per year.

If the same tenant's lease in the same shopping center provided for a calculation based on *leased and occupied basis*, and the shopping center was only 70% leased, the tenant's share would be 2,000/350,000, or 0.57%. On the same insurance premium, the tenant's billing would be $229 per year.

The difference is that on a leasable basis, the landlord is paying the pro-rata share of the insurance cost on the vacant spaces, but on a leased basis, the tenants are picking up all of the cost of the insurance and the landlord gets a full recovery.

Most shopping center leases charge the insurance on a leasable basis, and no extra administrative charges or supervision fees are added on to the cost of the premium. Make sure yours does it that way.

Insurance Billing in CAM

Some shopping center leases won't provide for a separate bill to the tenants for Property Insurance, but will add the expense of the insurance in as a Common Area Maintenance (CAM) expense, similar to the handling of liability insurance. The advantage to the landlord of handling it this way is that the landlord gets to collect the 15% admin fee assessed on the total CAM expenses, and gets to bill the tenants under the same formula as CAM, which is usually on a *leased and occupied* basis.

Many experienced tenants either exclude Insurance as a CAM item, or if it is going to be included in CAM, simply state that the 15% admin fee does not apply to the Insurance expense.

LIABILITY INSURANCE

Liability Insurance provides coverage in case someone is injured or property is damaged as a result of activities of the shopping center or the tenants. In most cases, the landlord in a shopping center provides liability insurance for the common areas, and the tenant provides liability insurance for its premises and its activities on the shopping center.

Shopping Center managers also require contractors and others doing work or performing other activities at the center to furnish proof of liability insurance.

TENANT BILLINGS FOR LIABILITY INSURANCE

Most shopping center leases require the landlord to provide liability insurance for the common areas of the shopping center, but the cost of that insurance is usually included in the Common Area Maintenance charges to the tenants on a "triple net" lease.

Most shopping center landlords typically charge a 15% supervision or administration fee on common area expenses before billing the costs back to the tenant, and the cost of the liability insurance is included in the 15% fee. Some national chain store tenants are successful in getting the cost of the insurance excluded from the 15% fee.

Most shopping center leases provide that the CAM expenses are billed to the tenants on a *leased and occupied* basis. Some tenants are successful in getting this lease clause changed to have liability insurance billed the same way as property insurance, without the 15% fee, and on a total GLA basis for calculating the pro-rata share.

Example: If the cost of liability insurance were $200,000 per year for a 500,000 SF shopping center that was 80% occupied, a tenant with 2,000 SF would pay the following for liability insurance in CAM:

500,000 x 80% = 400,000 SF

2,000 SF / 400,000 SF = 0.5% Pro-Rata Share

$200,000 premium cost x 115% = $230,000

$230,000 x 0.5% = $1,150.00 (Tenant's cost of the liability insurance in the CAM fee)

Now, if the same tenant in the same shopping center excluded the liability insurance from the CAM calculation and had it billed on a total leasable basis, the tenant would pay the following:

2,000 SF / 500,000 SF = 0.4% Pro-Rata Share

$200,000 premium cost x 0.4% = $800 (Tenant's cost of the liability insurance)

The tenant would save $350 per year on the cost of the liability insurance billing if the tenant could get the clause changed to have the liability insurance billed without the 15% admin fee and on a total leasable basis. Can you always get this changed? Probably not every time, but it's worth asking for.

INSURANCE CHECKLIST

☑ If the shopping center lease bills a separate charge for Property Insurance, try to get the insurance billing (INS) billed on a *total leasable area* basis, not on a *leased and occupied* area basis.

☑ Try to get the insurance expenses out of Common Area Maintenance (CAM) and have them billed separately on a pro-rata basis.

☑ If either or both types of insurance are handled in CAM and you can't get the landlord to bill it separately, then see if you can have the insurance expense excluded from the 15% admin fee in CAM.

☑ Most landlords will not agree to a cap on annual insurance increases, since they have no control over the insurance rates.

12

OTHER ADDITIONAL RENT EXPENSES

◆

Miscellaneous Fees Can Add Up

There have been separate sections on the additional rent expenses charged to the tenant for CAM, Real Estate Taxes and Insurance. In most shopping center leases there are other additional rent expenses that the tenant must pay. This chapter will describe a few of the more common 'additional rent' expenses.

HVAC CHARGES

There are different types of Heating, Ventilating and Air Conditioning (HVAC) systems in shopping centers. The simplest system is a rooftop mounted HVAC unit for each tenant space. This is usually the case in single-story shopping malls and strip centers. The tenant installs its own HVAC unit on the roof and maintains it. If the tenant were to move into a *second-generation* space, the tenant assumes the operation and maintenance (and/or replacement cost) of any existing HVAC equipment. There is no charge from the landlord in this case because the tenant controls, maintains and pays for its own HVAC expense, including electricity to run it.

In a multi-level shopping mall or other large facility, and sometimes in smaller malls, there is often a central HVAC system. There is a central plant or a large HVAC unit that supplies air to several stores in a zone of the shopping center. Each tenant space has some HVAC equipment to control the discharge of air into the tenant space. The equipment, such as a radiator or Variable Air Volume (VAV) box, is controlled by the tenant's own thermostat. Sometimes heat is provided within the landlord's air system, but often the heat is provided at the tenant space with electric heat coils in the air ducts of the tenant space. In large shopping centers, there is often a demand for cooling all year long due to heat produced by lights and warm bodies inside the enclosed mall. So, the landlord-supplied air is usually cool, and the individual tenants warm it a little with electric heat coils as needed. (The heating elements are normally wired to the tenant's electrical meter, so the tenant pays for the cost of electricity to heat the air).

If the shopping center has a central air conditioning system, and air is provided to the tenant space, the tenant will have to pay a share of the cost to operate and maintain the central air conditioning system. This is usually listed as a flat rate charge in the lease, but some leases simply say the tenant will pay for the cost of HVAC as determined by the landlord. It is a good idea to quantify that charge in the lease, and add a limit on how much it can increase each year. Otherwise, the tenant has no control over the amount charged by the landlord.

Another thing to watch for on an HVAC billing is the cost of capital replacements. If a tenant were to move into an older shopping mall and the air conditioning system was replaced in the second year of the tenant's lease term, the landlord may wish to increase the HVAC charge to the tenant to help pay for the capital cost of replacing the old equipment. The tenant's charge may very easily increase sharply without some control over the expense written into the lease.

Unlike taxes, insurance, and CAM, the charge for HVAC is typically not reconciled at the end of the year. The tenant just pays a flat rate charge to cover the cost of the HVAC service. In a large center that is well leased, the landlord can make a profit from the operation of the Central Plant.

CUMULATIVE AND NON-CUMULATIVE INCREASE CAPS

The difference between cumulative and non-cumulative increases is important. A non-cumulative increase means that the costs won't increase more than 5% for that one year compared to the prior year. A cumulative increase means the cap grows by 5% per year regardless of the actual increases each year.

Example of a *non-cumulative* 5% increase cap: Say the costs for a billing item started at $2.00 per square foot and increased 2% the first year, 3% the second year, and 8% the third year. Over a three-year period, the costs would increase to

$2.04, $2.10, and $2.27 PSF in the respective years. If the tenant had a lease provision limiting the annual increase to 5% on a non-cumulative basis, the increase in the third year would be limited to the 5% cap and the tenant would save the difference.

Example of a *cumulative* 5% increase cap: Say the costs for a billing item started at $2.00 per square foot at the commencement of the lease, and increased at the same as the above example—2%, 3% and 8%. Over a three-year period, the costs would increase to $2.04, $2.10, and $2.27 PSF in the respective years. The 5% cumulative cap would grow each year by 5% so starting at $2.00; the cap for the 3 years would be $2.10, $2.21, and $2.32. So even though there was an 8% increase in the third year, the cost would still be under a *cumulative 5% cap* so the tenant would have to pay the increase.

Over a long-term lease, the cumulative cap can grow much faster than the actual increase in expenses, resulting in no protection for the tenant from big increases in later years of the lease.

If the tenant requests a 5% cap on expenses, and if the landlord agrees, someone will try to make it a *cumulative cap*. If you don't understand the difference, you will not get the protection you are seeking for large increases in any one year.

ELECTRICITY CHARGES

Most shopping centers have individual electric meters installed by the local utility company, and the tenant pays the power used in its store directly to the utility company as metered. If a utility company individually meters your space, there is no charge from the landlord for power used in your space. You would still pay a share of electricity used in the common areas, and that is included in the CAM billing.

In some cases, such as for a kiosk, the kiosk is often wired to the "house" power and doesn't have a separate meter. In these cases, the landlord assesses a monthly power charge against the tenant. The charge is computed by determining how many watts of power the tenant's lighting and equipment uses, and then determining an average Kilowatt Hour used each month. In this case the tenant should ask that the lease provide for power to be charged at the same KWH rate that the local utility company charges.

There are some shopping centers that sub-meter the power to the tenants with landlord-controlled electric meters. The landlord representative may read the meter monthly and send the tenant a bill. In this case, the landlord is purchasing the power from the local utility company and 're-selling' it to the tenant. This can be a net profit center for the landlord. The tenant should make sure the lease provides for some control over the amount that is billed, and that there is some protection against power outages.

Check to see which way your shopping center handles the electricity for your store. If you are going to be billed by the landlord for the electricity, it is a good idea to make sure there is an electrical rate specified in the lease, and some language to control the eventual increases in costs. It is also important to make sure the rate the landlord charges is equivalent to the rate charged by the local utility company. There are often local laws regulating how much a landlord can "resell" power for, and in some jurisdictions there are laws prohibiting the resell of power by private parties, or at least making a profit on the resell. Finally, make sure that there is some provision in the lease to offer some protection in case landlord-supplied power is interrupted. You should try to get the rent to stop after approximately/about three days with no power.

TRASH CHARGES

In small strip shopping centers, the tenant may have to contract with a local trash hauling company and provide its own trash dumpster outside the back door. In that case, the landlord does not provide trash service for the tenant and there is no separate trash charge to the tenant, except for trash from the common areas, which is included in the CAM billing.

In large multi-tenant shopping centers it doesn't make sense for each little tenant to have its own separate trash container. There are usually central trash compactors operated by maintenance staff. In single level centers with rear doors, the mall may supply a trash dumpster outside in a nearby service area. The trash dumpster or cart is pulled to a central compactor and dumped and maintained by the mall's maintenance staff. In other properties, the tenants may have to take their trash to a central area via rear corridors and service elevators.

Larger shopping centers require tenants to separate the cardboard from the rest of the trash. Cardboard can be recycled and kept out of the landfill, thus decreasing the cost of the landfill fees. Some shopping centers may also have separate compactors for wet garbage from restaurants, and dry trash from retail stores.

The costs of collecting the trash, operating and maintaining the trash compactor, and the landfill fees are charged back to the tenants in some form. The method of handling trash charges varies with each shopping center. The simplest way, and probably the most common, is for the trash charges to be included in CAM, and for the tenants to pay for trash as part of their CAM expense. Since the CAM charges are allocated on a square footage basis, this method assumes that all tenants produce the same amount of trash, which is not always true.

Some landlords have attempted to set a separate trash charge in the lease, and account for the trash expenses separately. This is handled similar to the HVAC charge or Electricity charge, as a net profit center for the landlord. If this is the way it is handled in your center, make sure the rate you will be charged for trash is reasonable, and that the rate is set forth in the lease. Also make sure there is some control over future trash charge increases. If the compactor has to be replaced, the landlord may raise the trash charges to help pay for the capital expense of replacing the compactor. If this happens during your lease term, your trash rate could increase sharply.

If your lease puts trash into CAM, there should not be a separate trash charge with your monthly billing.

WATER AND SEWER CHARGES

If your space is in a small strip center property, you may have a separate water meter to just your space. In that case you will pay for water directly to the agency providing it. However, most retail users don't use a lot of water, and in larger centers it is common for a shared water meter. There is one large water main supplying water to the entire shopping center, or to a block of tenants within the shopping center.

For those spaces on a shared water meter, there are three ways the shopping center can handle the tenant billing:

1.   The most common way is to include the water in the CAM billing, and each tenant pays a pro-rata share of the total CAM expenses. This assumes that all tenants use the same amount of water per square foot, which isn't the case. If restaurants or hair salons are on the same meter,

the other tenants will be subsidizing their water usage because they use more water than a typical retail store, which just has a small restroom in the back.

2. The landlord can charge a PSF rate to each tenant on a separate billing. In this case, the rate that is charged could be higher for restaurants and other high-usage tenants, and lower for retail tenants.

3. The landlord can install a sub-meter on the water line going into the tenant space, and charge for the quantity used. This is the fairest way to do the billing, but because of the expense for separate meters, and the relatively low cost of water, it is seldom done.

As with the other utility charges, remember to make sure that the charge for the water is specified in the lease if there is a separate charge, and that there is some protection against future rate increases. The standard lease may say that the landlord has the right to sub-meter the water in the future. In that case, make sure the lease says that the metered rate does not exceed the rate charged by the local utility company.

UTILITY BILLINGS CHECKLIST

 For a shopping center lease with landlord-billed HVAC and/or utility charges, the tenant should have the charge stated in the lease, and make sure there is some control over increases in future years, such as a provision that costs will not increase more than 5% in any year, on a non-cumulative basis.

Always use a non-cumulative cap when getting a cap on rate increases. Don't agree to a cumulative cap.

MARKETING FEES

Almost all larger shopping centers and malls have some kind of a marketing assessment to the tenants to raise funds for advertising, promoting, and marketing the shopping center. In a strip center, this may be a small fee to pay for a small marketing budget for holiday decorations or a few ads during the year. But in a regional mall, the marketing budget can be several hundred thousand dollars a year, and the tenants pay a large monthly fee.

The marketing and promotion of a shopping center used to be handled by a Merchants Association, a separate non-profit corporation operated by the tenants in the shopping center. The lease required the tenant to join the Merchants Association and pay dues to the Association monthly. The dues were used to advertise and promote the center, and there was usually a group of tenants who served on a board of directors to work with the Marketing Director. There may still be some Merchants Associations around, but for the most part they have been replaced with a landlord-operated Marketing Fund.

The Merchants Associations were dissolved because most chain stores did not actively get involved in the associations. Chain stores don't do much local advertising, and chain store managers turn over frequently, so the Merchants Associations were not effective. The landlord-operated marketing program offers a simple, more professional approach to promoting the shopping center as an entity.

Typically, in larger properties, the landlord employs a professional Marketing Director at the shopping center to manage the marketing and promotions. In large centers, the director may have an assistant and a staff.

Marketing Fund

Whether the shopping center has a Merchants Association or a Marketing Fund, the tenants pay a lease-required monthly fee into a separate fund, and the funds are supposed to be used for marketing and promoting the shopping center. In most shopping center leases, the landlord agrees to participate in the Marketing Fund, usually as a matching funds contribution, although sometimes the landlord provides a professional Marketing Director in lieu of the cash contribution.

You should add a co-participation clause to the lease requirement to pay marketing fees, so that you are only required to pay if at least 75% of the other tenants in the shopping center are paying into the fund *at a similar rate*. You should add that the landlord would provide a list of tenants who are paying into the marketing fund upon tenant's request, about once a year. Even if you have the 75% requirement, the landlord likely won't monitor it for you and let you know if the participation rate falls below 75%. You'll have to check regularly.

It is also important to make sure the other tenants are paying at a similar rate. If you sign a lease and agree to pay $2.00 per square foot for a Marketing Fund, it is very likely that chain stores and national retailers have negotiated that down.

In a regional mall, find out what they are asking for the Marketing Fund, and then offer to pay one-half of the amounts they request. Landlords have had trouble getting tenants to participate in the Marketing Fund and the contribution rates have fallen way down.

Advertising Fund

There may be more than one charge in the lease related to marketing. Some shopping centers used to have a lease requirement that tenants participate in mall-sponsored advertising campaigns by purchasing a local ad. Since many mall chain stores do not want to advertise locally, this lease-required advertising has widely been replaced with a "Media Fund" or "Advertising Fund", which is an additional charge to the "Marketing Fund." The Advertising Fund is used to purchase advertising for the center to replace the old type of advertising where tenants were required to buy their own ads in a mall-sponsored advertising campaign.

If your lease has both an Advertising (Media) Fund and a Marketing Fund, you can try to get out of the Advertising (Media) Fund. If the funds have been commingled, it is likely they will let you out of the Media Fund. If the funds are still active and managed, and they really want you to pay into both funds, ask for a list of tenants who pay into both funds and the amounts they pay.

Both charges are often found in the pre-printed lease, but with some negotiation, most tenants can negotiate out of having to pay both marketing charges.

Grand Opening Assessment

If a new shopping center is opening, or if a shopping center is going through a redevelopment, the landlord will ask for a grand opening assessment, a one-time charge to the tenant to pay for the expenses of advertising and promoting a grand opening event for the shopping center. This is an additional charge, in addition to the Marketing Fund and Advertising Fund, and the tenant is required to pay upon opening.

If it truly is a new shopping center, it might be difficult to avoid paying the grand opening assessment. But if the center is already open, a tenant can usually get this clause removed.

CPI Increases

In most shopping center leases, the amount that the tenant pays into the Marketing Fund and Advertising Fund is increased annually by increases in the Consumer Price Index (CPI). These are modest annual increases, and serve to keep the total Marketing Fund viable. Without any annual increases, inflation would erode the buying power of the fund over time, and less advertising and promotional activities would result.

A tenant can usually ask for a not-to-exceed annual limit on the CPI increases. A cap of 5% in any one year is commonly inserted at the tenant's request.

Annual Marketing Budget

Larger shopping centers have a professional Marketing Director to handle the promotions and advertising for the center. Marketing expenses are incurred against an annual budget. The total amount of the budget is dependent on how much the tenants and the landlord contribute to the fund.

In most regional malls, there has been an erosion of the Marketing Fund budget in recent years, due to an increasing number of national tenants refusing to participate in the fund. The national retailers claim that the center's marketing efforts do them little good, and they would rather spend the money promoting their own businesses. As the Marketing budget decreases, many landlords have decided to increase their contribution to the fund to help bolster the funds, but some budgets have suffered.

You should agree to the payments to the Marketing Fund, but *only so long as* a majority of the other tenants are paying to the fund in a similar amount per square foot. If the fund gets so low that the only ones left paying into it are a few local small tenants, the budget won't be large enough to accomplish anything. You don't want that to happen, and be one of the last ones paying into it. If you are going into a shopping center you should support the fund within reason, but only as long as the national retailers are supporting it. Make sure to leave yourself an 'out' if the fund dwindles.

You don't want to be the last one paying into a watered down meager fund that doesn't have a large enough budget to accomplish its purposes.

MARKETING FEES CHECKLIST

☑ Get out of the Grand Opening Assessment unless it is a new shopping center and a new grand opening is planned. Pay a grand opening assessment only if at least 75% of the other tenants are also paying a similar amount.

☑ If there are two separate charges for "Marketing or Promotion Fund" and "Advertising or Media Fund", get the Advertising Fund *deleted*. Practically the only tenants left paying for both charges are small business owners who haven't caught on yet.

☑ Make sure that you add a co-participation clause in the lease that says you will pay into the Marketing Fund *only if 75% of the other tenants* in the shopping center are actively paying into the fund *at the same or higher rates* than you are paying.

☑ Ask the landlord to provide an annual schedule of other tenants paying into the Marketing Fund upon your request, perhaps at the end of each year with the CAM settlement.

☑ Get a cap on the annual Marketing Fee increase per the Consumer Price Index, such as not to exceed 5% in any year.

13

SPECIAL LEASE PROVISIONS

✦

Shopping Center Leases Are Written To Benefit the Landlord

The standard shopping center lease won't have a lot of special provisions that benefit the tenant. You have to request these provisions and ask for them to be written into the standard lease, or on an attached rider. Don't be afraid to ask for any special provisions—don't assume the standard pre-printed lease is the same for everyone. It's not. Most sophisticated tenants get many special provisions written into the lease. You may not be able to get as many as a national chain store with a strong credit rating, but you should be able to get some of the following provisions to protect your business interests.

EXCLUSIVES

An *Exclusive* refers to an Exclusive Use Provision, where the landlord guarantees that it will not lease space to any other tenant that sells the same type of goods for which the tenant has an exclusive. Examples might include a McDonald's restaurant, where the landlord gives the McDonald's tenant an exclusive that no other tenant in the shopping center can sell hamburgers. Thereafter, the landlord would have to limit the use of each new tenant to make sure they were not authorized to sell hamburgers. Sometimes, there are exclusives for a certain number of similar stores within the same shopping center. For example, an athletic shoe store might have a lease provision that says the landlord will not lease space to more than 3 athletic shoe stores. With this type of provision, there is still an opportunity for the shopping center to remain competitive by leasing space to 3 similar operators, but not over saturate the one category.

Most shopping center managers avoid giving exclusives to any tenant unless it is absolutely necessary to make a lease deal. Most often, when an exclusive is found, it is for a large national tenant for a limited, specific use. Small tenants are seldom given an exclusive. Why? The shopping center cannot afford to give away a whole category of merchandise for a small tenant, especially if the tenant is unproven. Customers like to shop and they will go where the best retailers are. If, over time, a shopping center ended up with several under-performing, worn-out retailers with exclusive uses, the shopping center would suffer as customers went elsewhere, and the manager of the shopping center was limited to bring in new tenants. A fact of life in shopping centers is that retail is a competitive business.

It is highly unlikely that you can get an exclusive in a prominent shopping center unless it is for a very specific one-of-a-kind use.

KICK-OUTS

A *Kick-Out* refers to a lease provision where either the landlord or the tenant, or both, may terminate the lease at some future time if some future condition is not met. Kick-outs are usually tied to sales performance. A tenant might negotiate a new lease with a special provision that if the store's sales do not exceed $300,000 in year 2, then the tenant has the option to terminate the lease at the end of the second year. This is some built-in protection for the tenant in case the store doesn't take off.

Sometimes a landlord will have a kick-out also, where the landlord can terminate a tenant's lease after a few years if the tenant is not performing adequately. Get this clause deleted.

If you are starting a new lease you absolutely should try to get a kick-out. This is insurance for a later day, in case the business fails. Anything can happen to knock a retail store's sales off: new competition opens, existing anchor stores close, the concept just didn't work, suppliers went out of business, major illness of the owner, economic conditions, etc. It is a lot easier to negotiate a kick-out up front than it is to try to negotiate a lease termination at a later date, perhaps when you have fallen on hard times. A kick-out allows you to get out of the lease as a worst-case scenario. It also gives you a lever to renegotiate the lease later if you need to.

Get the kick-out provision based on sales performance. Sometimes, a landlord will want the tenant to repay any lease commissions, tenant improvement allowance, and other costs the landlord might have incurred to make the deal. If you run into that, don't agree to any payback. As a last resort, at least get an agreement to calculate the payback based on an *amortized* repayment plan, where the costs are amortized over the lease term, and you pay only the unamortized (or pro-rated) amount left.

Many national chain stores are insisting on kick-outs now. They have had too many experiences where they have gotten sucked into an under performing shopping center, and couldn't get out. To avoid having a number of those bad locations drag the entire chain's profitability down, they get a kick-out provision as a safeguard.

CO-OCCUPANCY

A *Co-Occupancy Provision* refers to a lease clause where certain other tenants are also required to be open (co-occupants). Since the major anchor tenants of a shopping center are the draw that keeps the center viable, if a major tenant closes it can be devastating on a small business. Without any protection against such an event, you are stuck with a long-term lease at high rents and there is nothing much to do about it.

Usually a Co-occupancy provision will refer to an anchor tenant, or more than one anchor tenant being open, but the provision can also include certain other tenants, or a requirement that a percentage of the shopping center space must be open.

There are various remedies for a co-occupancy failure. In some cases, the tenant's lease simply says the tenant is only required to be open when the anchor stores are open or, say, 70% of the other stores are open. The only remedy here is that the tenant is not required to open—to "go dark"—*but the tenant still has to pay rent.* This is not much protection for you. Be careful of this—many landlords will offer this to an unknowing tenant figuring that the tenant won't understand the difference.

The remedy for failure to meet a co-occupancy requirement should allow the tenant the option to terminate the lease if the co-occupancy requirement is not met. This provides insurance for the tenant against the worst-case scenario, similar to the kick-out provision.

In some Co-occupancy provisions, the landlord will ask for a *cure period* of 6 months to a year, to give them time to find a replacement anchor or bring the center occupancy up above the required level. In this case, the tenant should negotiate for the option to pay percentage rent only during the cure period as a remedial rent. Then, if sales fall off, the rent will be reduced.

Another common remedy in a co-occupancy clause doesn't allow the tenant to terminate the lease, but allows the tenant to pay percentage rent in lieu of the base rent during the time the co-occupancy requirement is not met. This is better than nothing, but the right to terminate is better. If you have the right to terminate and something happens, you can always negotiate a lease amendment for percentage rent. But if your only remedy is to pay percentage rent, you don't have the better option to terminate.

The best possible remedy for the tenant would be a clause that allows the tenant to have the option to either terminate the lease or stay and pay percentage rent, if desired. Say a major anchor tenant in the shopping center closed. Over the next few months, customer traffic fell off and sales dropped. If the only remedy were to terminate the lease and vacate, the tenant might be forced to do that. But say the landlord is working with a replacement anchor store that will open a year later. Perhaps it would make sense to pay a lower rent and struggle along for a year, and still be in business when the new anchor store opens.

Negotiate for the co-occupancy requirement, and tie it to the major anchor tenant(s) in the shopping center *and* a certain percentage of other shop space open, say 60% to 70%. Get a remedy that allows the tenant the option to terminate or stay and pay percentage rent.

CAPS ON CAM FEES

A *Cap* refers to a limit on how much can be charged for fees such as Common Area Maintenance (CAM). Costs of operating a shopping center can increase dramatically, especially if the center is older and there are many things that need to be replaced or renovated. Many landlords will try to recover from the tenants through CAM as much of the costs as possible.

There are different types of caps on CAM. The simplest one is to set a rate in the lease and have a special provision that the rate won't increase more than 5% in any one year (non-cumulative). This offers some protection against spiking CAM costs in any particular year.

Other types of caps on CAM deal with the tenant's share of the CAM costs. There are two things that affect a tenant's CAM cost:

- The actual expenses of operating the shopping center, and
- The number of tenants who share the expenses (the pro-rata share).

The Pro-Rata Share of CAM Expenses

It is a good idea to negotiate a special provision in the lease to limit the pro-rata share the tenant pays. If the shopping center lost a lot of tenants over time, and the CAM costs were shared by fewer and fewer tenants, the cost for each tenant would get higher and higher. The best deal is to get a lease that computes the CAM pro-rata share for the tenant based on the total square footage of the shopping center (referred to as a 100% denominator). If that won't work, at least try to get a limit of, say, 75% or 80% minimum. If the occupancy falls below 75%, the tenant's pro-rata share will still be based on 75%.

Sometimes, savvy shopping center managers will want to exclude some CAM expenses from the cap, for things that are outside of the manager's control. Expenses such as real estate taxes on the common area, liability insurance, and even snow removal are dependent on outside circumstances and are not entirely within the manager's control. Don't bring this up—let them negotiate their own lease—but if they insist on a "line item veto", some caps are better than none.

Actual CAM Expense Increases

Whenever possible, the tenant should negotiate for a cap on how much the CAM expenses can increase each year. The best deal, of course, is to get two caps: a not-to-exceed limit on expenses, and a limit on the pro-rata share. It's possible, and getting more and more common.

Be careful how a 'growth rate' cap is worded. If it is a cumulative growth cap of 5% per year, in a few short years, it is worthless protection. You want a non-cumulative cap that limits the increase of CAM costs in any one year, irrespective of what happened in earlier years.[1]

For example, if a tenant has a lease with a special provision for a CAM cap that is worded something like this: "At the commencement of this lease, tenant's CAM expenses shall not exceed $6.00 PSF, and this cap shall increase 5% per year." In the 5th year of the lease, the tenant's cap on the CAM expenses would have grown to $7.66 PSF. If actual CAM costs during the first four years of the lease term had increased only an average of 1.5% per year, the actual costs would be at $6.37 PSF, well under the cap, which has been growing 5% per year. In the 5th year (or any year), the shopping center could jump the CAM billing up to the $7.66 cap, *a one-year jump of 20.25%.*

Get the cap on a year-to-year basis, not a cumulative cap that grows every year. Make sure it is spelled out so it can be easily understood in the lease. There is often a lot of ambiguity in these types of special provisions, simply because the people writing the leases don't fully understand it.

SPECIAL LEASE PROVISIONS CHECKLIST

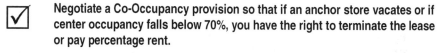 **Negotiate a kick-out based on sales performance so that you have the right to terminate the lease in future years if sales fall below a minimum level.**

☑ **Negotiate a Co-Occupancy provision so that if an anchor store vacates or if center occupancy falls below 70%, you have the right to terminate the lease or pay percentage rent.**

☑ **Get two caps on the CAM expenses—one to limit your pro-rata share of the expenses, such as a ratio based on the total leasable area instead of the open and occupied area—and one to limit the annual increase of CAM costs, such as a non-cumulative cap of 5% in any one year.**

---

1.   See the Chapter on CAM for a complete description of Cumulative and Non-Cumulative Caps

14

LEASE CLAUSES

✦

Understand All the Lease Clauses Before Signing

There are many lease clauses affecting a small tenant in a shopping center. Before signing a lease, make sure you are comfortable with all of the clauses. Always seek legal advice on any question about a lease agreement. The following just describes a few of the lease clauses that affect the operation of a small business. It is not a comprehensive list of all clauses in a lease, many of which have important legal considerations. Always seek legal advice to get an opinion on any lease agreement.

ASSIGNMENT OF LEASE

This clause is important in case you want to sell the business someday. In all shopping center leases, the lease is not assignable to a buyer without the landlord's specific approval. Some leases will spell out what is going to be necessary to obtain the landlord's consent to an assignment of the lease, but other leases are silent. Make sure your lease sets forth the criteria for the landlord to approve an assignment. For example, some leases will state that an assignee must have a similar net worth and similar business experience as the assignor. At least with this kind of language in the lease, you have an argument to get the lease assigned to a buyer.

There may be some cases where you may want to perform certain types of transfers of ownership, such as stock transfers, or assigning the lease to a subsidiary company, without the landlord's approval. This is easily accomplished by adding a paragraph to the assignment clause, to allow certain transfers without obtaining the landlord's approval and without an assignment of the lease. This is routinely done.

Most leases require the tenant to submit a fee to pay for the landlord's legal costs of preparing the lease assignment document. You should get a "not to exceed" limit in there, say, $500 to $700. Otherwise, they can charge you what they want to.

LEASE TERM AND LEASE DATES

Each shopping center lease has several key dates:

Lease Date. This is just a reference date for the document. The lease is usually dated when it is signed.

Lease Term Start Date. This is the commencement date in the lease, when the lease term actually starts. The commencement date for most shopping center leases is the first day of the month after the day the tenant opens for business. That way, the term always starts on a whole month.

Rent Start Date: Usually there is an outside date when the tenant must open and start paying rent, called the Required Commencement Date (RCD). This date often trips up tenants resulting in needless extra costs. When a new tenant starts negotiating a lease there is optimism about when they can open. Often, the tenant agrees to a commencement date, which seems at the time a long way off. But as the length of time drags on to get the lease negotiated, reviewed, get store plans done, contractor bids, and so on, the tenant doesn't open until long after the RCD. The lease says rent starts when the tenant opens, or the RCD, whichever is sooner. So, the tenant now has a problem and has to start paying rent before the business opens. The way to avoid this is to keep moving that RCD back to make sure you have more than enough time to get the store open before rent starts. Add more time than you think is necessary. If the landlord won't agree to a stretched-out date, then change it from a firm date to "90 days after the landlord signs and delivers the lease to the tenant", or "90 days after landlord approves tenant construction plans", or something similar.

End Date: This is when the lease ends. Most leases are worded so that the term of the lease starts on the first day of the month after the date the tenant opens for business (or on the Required Commencement Date). Thus, the lease ends on the last day of the month when the lease term runs out. If the tenant opens on a five-year lease on May 17th, the lease term starts on June 1st, and ends on May 31st, five years later.

A retail tenant should want the lease to end on a specific time of the year, such as January 31st, so the tenant can stay through the busy Holiday season at the end of the lease term, have a January clearance sale, and have time to close the store. Many tenants open a retail store in the fall, just before the Holidays. If you don't change the ending date, your lease will end when it began—just before the Holiday season. If you have a retail store, don't let the lease terminate on November 30th, or some other date where you wouldn't want to close the store, or be held up for high rents during the final month. You can always add a fixed ending date in the lease—it doesn't have to be for whole numbers of years or months.

LEASABLE AREA

The shopping center leases define the tenant's leasable area in square feet. The square footage in a shopping center lease is determined with the following measurements:

Measurements are taken from the *outside edge* of an outside wall. If there is a rear wall in the space, add 8" to the inside measurement for a cinderblock wall.

In an enclosed mall, measurements are taken from the lease line at the storefront. In some shopping centers, the lease line provides for a 2-foot pop out on the front of the store, and the measurement is taken from the outer edge of the pop out. This is the case, even if the tenant doesn't build all the way out to the pop out. For example, if a tenant builds a protruding canopy over the storefront, the lease line would be the outer edge of the canopy.

Measurements are taken to the centerline of a shared wall between two tenant spaces. If there is a 2x6 wall separating two spaces, add 3 to 4 inches to the inside measurement.

In almost all cases, two people can measure the same space and get a slightly different measurement. The lease defines the square footage of the premises to avoid disputes later on over the size of the space. If in doubt, measure before you sign the lease. Remember that the size of the space in the lease will be larger than your usable size because of the thickness of the walls, and outer edge measurements.

USE OF PREMISES

The Use Clause in a shopping center lease describes what the tenant may use the premises for. This clause is important. Make sure it accurately describes what items or services will be sold from the premises, and be as complete as possible. Some use clauses are very long paragraphs, a half-page or more.

Don't be confused—the use clause is NOT an *exclusive use clause*. The use clause describes what the tenant can sell—it gives no promises or guarantees that other tenants in the shopping center can't sell the same thing. Exclusives are rarely given.

COMMON AREA USE

Shopping Center leases say that the landlord can use the common areas for nearly any purpose, including leasing space to carts and kiosks. Some tenants like to insert a clause in the lease that the landlord cannot place a kiosk or cart, or other similar type of display, within so many feet of the tenant's storefront. This is to avoid having a large kiosk placed in front of the tenant's store that blocks the view and access to the store. If this might be a problem in your location, see what kind of wording you can insert into the lease to keep your entrance and window displays visible and open.

RELOCATION

Most shopping center leases allow the landlord to relocate the tenant at any time. Read this clause carefully. If at some point in time you are about to be relocated and you don't like the space that is being proposed, what remedy do you have? Make sure the relocation language in the lease provides for your approval of the substitute location, or allows you the right to cancel the lease if you don't like the new location.

If you are only interested in the location you are leasing, such as the end location in a strip mall, with full exposure to the street, then you probably won't agree to any relocation. Try to get the relocation clause deleted.

If you can't get the relocation clause deleted, try to tighten it up by adding some extra provisions, such as the landlord can only relocate you if there is going to be a significant redevelopment of the shopping center. Also, try to get a requirement that the landlord will reimburse you for the costs of your Tenant Improvements, and the costs of moving, including the soft costs of stationary, business cards, etc.

RADIUS RESTRICTION

The shopping center lease will have a restriction on the tenant from opening a store within a large radius, probably 5 miles or so. The penalty if the radius clause is violated is that the tenant must add the sales from both stores to determine the percentage rent due.

If there is ever any likelihood that you may want to ever open a similar business, change the radius clause (or delete it). Most landlords will agree to lower the radius limit for a smaller tenant to, say, 1 mile. This can be an important clause if business conditions change.

Tenants whose business is based on impulse goods or fast food should try to get out of the radius clause completely. These are not the same as a destination business where the radius clause might be more applicable.

For example, if you own a cookie store, don't agree to a radius clause of 5 miles. What if you have an opportunity to open another outlet a mile or so away at a different shopping center? Is that outlet going to take away sales from your existing store? That's doubtful. But if you agree to the radius clause in the first lease, you can't open the second store and you miss out on an opportunity to grow your business.

IMPROVEMENTS & REMODELING

The shopping center lease requires the tenant to get the landlord's approval before any significant remodeling work is done. Usually, there is a dollar limit set in the lease to define when the tenant has to get approval, but often the dollar limit is very low, such as $2,000. It is not unreasonable to raise that dollar limit to, say, $10,000 or more so the tenant doesn't have to go through a lengthy approval process and pay for design fees and mailing fees to get a fairly simple remodel project approved.

There will be an exhibit attached to the shopping center lease describing what work is the landlord's and what work is the tenant's. If the tenant is going to ask the landlord to do some work to the premises, make sure the work is itemized in the lease, or in the construction exhibit.

GUARANTOR

If a corporation signs a lease, the landlord will usually want one or more of the officers or principals to personally guarantee the lease. If the corporation has significant assets and a proven history, sometimes the principals can get out of a personal guarantee. Likewise, if the tenant is a person with no assets or personal worth, the landlord may require another party to guarantee the lease.

The guarantor personally signs that he/she will pay the rent and other obligations if the tenant doesn't pay. This guarantee extends for the length of the lease, and possible *for any extensions.* If you are guaranteeing a lease, try to get out of the extended lease terms—try to have the guarantee for a limited time, like the first 3 years of the lease term. If you just sign the guarantee, and the business is later sold, and the lease is extended, your obligation can drag on a long time into the future.

If you are a guarantor on a lease, and the business is sold, try to get off the guarantee as soon as possible. In most cases you can at least limit the guarantee period to the original term of the lease, so if the person buying the business later extends the lease you won't be on the hook for the extended terms.

It is unlikely that a start-up small business can get a lease in the name of a newly created shell corporation. Almost always, the business owner will have to personally guarantee the lease. However, you can always present the lease proposal with the name of the corporation as the tenant, and let the landlord ask for the personal guarantee. You can then use your agreement to a personal guarantee as a bargaining chip to get something from the landlord that will benefit you, such as a kick-out.

TENANT CERTIFICATES OF INSURANCE

The shopping center leases require the tenant to furnish proof of insurance to the landlord, and require the tenant to name the landlord as an *additional insured* under the tenant's policy.

Most leases will require the tenant to maintain $2 Million or more in liability insurance. Often, you can have the limit reduced to $1 Million or $2 Million if the lease requires more.

The lease will also require the tenant to maintain 80% to 100% Property Insurance on the Tenant Improvements and inventory. Again, most tenants can get this requirement down to 80% if the lease says 100%.

The lease may also require air conditioning insurance if the tenant has a large boiler or other machinery, and the lease may require liquor liability insurance if the tenant serves alcohol.

The tenant will have to purchase a policy of insurance from an insurance company, and make sure that the insurance agent provides the *Certificate of Insurance*, along with the *Additional Insured Endorsement* to the shopping center manager. The Certificate of Insurance shows that a policy is in place and gives the basic policy details The Additional Insured endorsement lists the entities that are insured under the tenant's policy, in addition to the tenant. Typically, the landlord will need to be on the list, along with the shopping center manager. Possibly the major anchor stores or the mortgage lender will also need to be added to the list.

Some insurance policies are now charging for the Additional Insured Endorsements, and for each Certificate of Insurance that is sent out. Check on these costs ahead of time when getting bids on your insurance policies.

LEASE CLAUSES CHECKLIST

☑ Always seek legal advice on any lease agreement.

☑ Change the assignment clause to make sure you have some reasonable ways to assign the lease in the event you ever want to sell your business.

☑ Add the document fee cost as a not-to-exceed price to process lease assignments, lease amendments, etc.

☑ Make sure the Required Commencement Date is set far enough away to give you plenty of time to get the store open.

☑ Get protection against kiosks or other obstructions in front of your store.

☑ Reduce the radius clause for other business locations, or get it deleted entirely.

☑ Try to negotiate as much as possible on your personal guarantee exposure.

15

THE LEASE NEGOTIATION PROCESS

◆

Patience is a Virtue

The negotiation process for a shopping center lease is more complicated than you think. For a busy shopping center, it can take weeks and months from the time you present a lease proposal to finally getting your signed lease in the mail. It is helpful to understand the process and the players.

THE LEASE PROPOSAL & THE BUSINESS DEAL

All lease deals begin with a written lease proposal. Sometimes the landlord's leasing representative writes the proposal, but you are better off writing your own proposal. The leasing agent won't put everything in the proposal that you would put in, so write your own proposal.

The lease proposal is often referred to as the 'business deal' because it has the basic business terms that were offered. It is often referred to as a 'letter of intent'. The proposal is usually in the form of a letter, simply listing the terms and conditions under which you would be willing to sign a lease for a space. You should list almost everything that you want to see in the lease in the proposal letter.

Later in the lease process when you are having trouble getting all of your clauses covered the way you want them in the lease, you can go back and refer to your letter and say, "The original business deal was this." If you don't have your terms written down on a proposal, you have less leverage to get that final approval and acceptance.

Although the proposal letter isn't binding on either you or the landlord, it is very helpful to have the terms of the business deal in writing. Many times, the lease document has some gray areas where the writer of the lease didn't make a point clear. Occasionally, the original business terms listed in the proposal letter come into play to resolve what the lease was supposed to have made clear.

Notice that the proposal letter simply outlines the terms in brief form. The lease will have language to clarify and explain each term more fully, and the lease document will need to be read carefully to make sure it says what was intended.

SAMPLE BUSINESS PROPOSAL

Date

Leasing Agent
Landlord
Address

Re: Name of Shopping Center

Dear Leasing Agent:

This will confirm my proposal to enter into a lease under the following terms and conditions:

Shopping Center:	Name of Shopping Center, City, State
Space:	Space Number
Size:	2,000 SF Gross Leasable Area
Tenant:	Retail Company, Inc., a (State) LLC
Use:	For the retail sale of (itemized list of products)
Base Rent:	$14 PSF per year for years 1–3
	$15 PSF per year for years 4–5
Term:	5 years and 4 months, commencing on October 1, 2004 and terminating on January 31, 2010
Overage Rent:	6%, natural breakpoints, commencing in the calendar year 2005. No overage rent is due for the partial year of 2004.
	Overage rent to be paid monthly after the breakpoint is reached.
Rent Concession:	Base rent for the first 3 full months and any partial month at the beginning of the lease term shall be waived.
	Percentage rent at the rate of 6% of sales shall be paid in lieu of base rent for the 4th through 6th month of the lease term.
	The fixed Base Rent shall begin the 7th full month of the term.

CAM: Pro-rata share of CAM to be determined on a total leasable area basis (100% GLA). Increases in CAM limited to 5% in any one year on a non-cumulative basis.

                     CAM fee at commencement shall be $8.00 PSF per year.

RE Taxes & Ins.: Pro-rata share of Real Estate Taxes and Insurance to be determined on a total leasable area basis (100% GLA). No supervision or administration fee on taxes or insurance.

Marketing Fund: $1.00 PSF per year, subject to annual CPI increases not to exceed 5% in any year. Participation conditioned on 75% of other tenants in the shopping center also participating at similar rates.

                     No advertising requirement. No media fund or advertising fund payments.

Utilities: Electricity metered by power company. Landlord to provide water, sewer and trash as part of CAM expense.

Sales Kick-out: If tenant sales do not exceed $400,000 in any calendar year after the second full calendar year of the lease term, tenant may cancel the lease.

Co-Occupancy: If *Major Department Store* and *Major Anchor Store* close for business, or if less than 75% of the GLA of the other non-anchor store space is not open, then tenant may have the option to either terminate the lease or pay remedial rent of 6% in lieu of base rent.

Tenant Improve: Landlord to provide tenant with an allowance of $30 PSF for tenant improvements to the space.

This proposal is subject to the final approval of all parties, and is not binding on either party. This proposal may be changed or withdrawn at any time.

Sincerely,

Tenant

THE DEAL APPROVAL PROCESS

Initially, you will deal with a leasing agent or property manager. You will negotiate, discuss and go back and forth until you are ready to submit a proposal.

You may go back and forth several times with a proposal letter before you finally
have a deal the leasing agent thinks can be accepted. The leasing agent will likely
want to negotiate a little with you over some of the terms of the lease, so always
allow yourself some negotiating room in your initial proposal to make counter
offers. Eventually, the leasing agent will have to submit the proposal to a senior
manager, or perhaps to a landlord representative for additional approvals.

Large shopping center management companies may have 3 or 4 layers of management that have to approve new lease deals. The process may take a few weeks,
especially if it goes back for changes. Many large, national companies now have
computer networks that are used to obtain approvals electronically, to avoid
sending paper documents all over the country. This seems like it should speed the
process up, but it hasn't. Approvals take a long time.

When it comes back to you with changes keep working to get the best terms you
can. Don't give up and cave in, although it is always a good strategy to let some
things go in exchange for other concessions.

After the deal is approved, it goes to a lease administrator or a legal person to pre-
pare a document.

THE LEASE DOCUMENT

The lease document is always prepared by the landlord's lease administrator or by
the landlord's law firm. A paralegal or an assistant under the supervision of a real
estate attorney will probably draft the actual document. They almost always make
mistakes, so don't panic when you get your lease and some things were left out or
poorly written.

In most cases, the landlord sends out a 'draft' copy of a lease for the tenant to
review. You are not expected to sign the draft copy—you are expected to read it,
have an attorney read it, and make any comments you want in the completed
lease document.

This is where most small owners make the biggest mistake of the whole leasing process. They accept the standard pre-printed lease agreement as it is presented and make no comments or changes to it. In a shopping center manager's office there are files of leases. It is easy to tell the leases that are with small business owners—they are the ones that have nice clean, white pages with no changes, additions or deletions. The leases that are negotiated by industry professionals are marked up on nearly every page.

This is your opportunity to sit down with the lease draft and a copy of this manual and go through the lease document with a marking pen. Attach paragraphs, line things out, attach riders and pages, and word the lease the way you want it worded, so that you have some protection as discussed throughout this manual. It is often a good idea to meet with the leasing agent or property manager to discuss the lease draft and your changes, so they are aware of what you want. Also, it is always a good idea to get your lawyer to read through the lease and make sure you are protected.

Send the marked-up draft back to the paralegal that sent it to you. Some of the changes you requested will be routine, and the paralegal will have authority to go ahead and accept your changes. Some of your changes will likely have to be reviewed for approval. If senior management has an issue with any of the changes, or if they are outside the terms of the approved deal, then it will likely go back to the leasing agent, who will be assigned to come talk to you. This is where it will have been important to have the business deal outlined in your proposal, to show that you aren't changing the deal, just clarifying what you want. They don't like it when you change the terms of the business deal and if you try to do that, it will really slow things down.

The legal person almost always tries to get a better deal for the landlord. Perhaps it is their competitive nature, but they will seldom give you everything you ask for, or will try to re-word what you want to thin it down and make it less of a deal for you and a better deal for the landlord. Just recognize that they work for the landlord and hold your ground.

After you have gone back and forth with the paralegal on several points, the paralegal will send you completed leases to be signed. There may be several copies of the lease to be executed. Make sure you are careful about signing the leases correctly and getting witnesses or notaries as required by law in your jurisdiction.

YOUR ATTORNEY

It is always a good idea to have an attorney represent you during the lease documentation process. They can read the various clauses and make sure you have reasonable protections. Attorney fees are expensive so it is a good idea to go to an attorney experienced in shopping center leases. If you go to an attorney who has never seen a shopping center lease before, you will be paying a lot of money for the attorney to get familiar with the industry and the leases used.

The landlord's attorney or paralegal would much prefer to work with a tenant's attorney than directly with the tenant. If both of them are professionals, they can quickly and neatly get a lease finished.

THE SIGNED LEASE

After you have signed the lease documents and sent them back to the paralegal, it may take some time to have the leases signed by the landlord's representative. After the leases are finally executed, you will usually be mailed a copy of the signed lease.

Keep your lease in a safe location. Review it from time to time, perhaps annually, to see if there are any terms or deadlines that you need to pay attention to.

CERTIFICATES AND ESTOPPELS

After you have signed the lease and opened your store, you will likely be asked to sign a certificate stating that the lease has commenced and that there are no issues left to be handled, and that the rent is accruing and so on.

Occasionally during the lease term you may be asked to sign an estoppel certificate. This is usually done if the shopping center is refinanced or sold. The estoppel shows the rent you are paying, the terms of the lease, and requires you to state if there are any disputes or defaults under the lease. These are routine, but you may want to seek legal advice if there are any clauses or statements in the estoppel you aren't comfortable signing.

LEASE PROCESS CHECKLIST

☑ **Make a written proposal to get all your business terms into the deal.**

☑ **Make changes to the lease draft per the suggestions and checklists in this manual.**

16

TENANT IMPROVEMENTS

✦

Landlords Do Not Usually Build Stores For Shopping Center Tenants

The term *Tenant Improvements (TI)* refers to the building and construction work necessary to build out a tenant space for the tenant's use. Shopping centers don't build the stores for the tenants. The tenant has to build out the leased premises to suit the needs of the tenant. Each tenant store is different, and has its own unique style and appearance, so landlords don't usually build out the stores for the retail tenants.

WHAT DO THE LANDLORDS BUILD?

The landlord of a shopping center typically provides the shell construction only—bare stud walls called demising walls, which separate one tenant space from another, concrete floor, roof, and basic utility lines to the premises. The tenant takes it from there—putting in walls, ceilings, air conditioning, stock rooms, flooring, lighting, plumbing, and all other improvements to the space to make it a finished retail store. At the end of the lease term, all of the tenant improvements stay with the space. The tenant can only take its movable trade fixtures out of the premises and cannot remove anything that is built in or attached.

VANILLA SHELL BUILD-OUTS

A typical strip shopping center initially provides a few more improvements than just the shell construction. The following improvements are often built by the landlord, and are referred to as a "vanilla shell": a glass storefront, sheetrock walls taped but not painted, concrete floor, drop-in ceiling with fluorescent lighting, fire sprinklers, a restroom, and probably an HVAC unit on the roof. This type of finished tenant space is sometimes referred to as a "vanilla shell", and the tenant is responsible for all improvements to the space from there.

A newly built enclosed mall initially provides only a bare space with bare studs for the demising walls for the first tenant to occupy the space. The landlord typically provides: a water line stubbed into the space, empty conduit lines for utilities stubbed in, a bare concrete floor, no storefront, no ceiling, no restrooms, and no HVAC unless it is on a shared system. The tenant is responsible for all improvements to the space, including the HVAC if it is a separate unit, fire sprinklers, and all interior improvements. The cost for you to build out a mall store is substantially more expensive than for a typical strip shopping center.

EXISTING IMPROVEMENTS

After a tenant has initially built a space out, when that tenant leaves, all of the tenant improvements stay behind. This is referred to as a *second-generation* space. A second (or third or fourth) tenant following behind may use the improvements that are there, or may remodel the existing improvements to suit its needs, or may tear everything out and start over. If you can find a suitable second-generation space and recycle the improvements you can save substantially on the cost of building a store.

National chain tenants don't usually recycle second-generation improvements. If they are leasing second-generation space, they almost always will demolish any existing improvements and rebuild the store to suit their needs. They may save the sheetrock on some of the demising walls, or perhaps a restroom, but they usually tear everything out and start over with all new improvements, equipment and furnishings. Each tenant has its own type of store, with an identifying image and design, and assigns little or no value to a previous tenant's improvements. Strong national retailers will remodel stores every 10 years or so in the same manner—tear everything out and redo the store completely. Some landlords demand complete store remodels when a tenant extends a lease; otherwise the shopping center would end up with old, stale stores.

Even though most national chain retailers build new stores, you can save a lot of money by finding a suitable location with some existing tenant improvements that can be re-used. You can adapt some generic type of improvements and make them work. However, almost every space will need at least some remodel work, and the cost of the remodel can be expensive. Where possible, you should try to negotiate to get as much help from the landlord as possible.

TENANT ALLOWANCE

The standard shopping center lease requires the tenant to be responsible for all the tenant improvement costs of construction. Twenty years ago, it was unusual for a landlord to give a tenant an allowance to build out the store. The landlord built the shopping center, and the tenants built their stores. The situation has changed in recent years. Most tenants going into regional enclosed malls get a tenant allowance. Some get a very high allowance. Most tenants in strip shopping centers also get an allowance.

The *Tenant Allowance (TA)* is the amount of money the landlord will contribute to the tenant for use on the construction costs of the tenant improvements. The TA is usually paid to the tenant *after* the improvements are completed and paid for, and the tenant has to show proof of payment to the contractors and suppliers (lien waivers). Sometimes, a tenant can negotiate progress payments of the tenant allowance, but it usually takes so long for a shopping center management company to process a payment request, the construction is done before the first payment arrives. So, in a typical tenant allowance arrangement, the tenant must be financially strong enough to cover the costs of the construction before getting reimbursed by the landlord under the tenant allowance agreement.

An alternative to a tenant allowance is to have the landlord do some of the tenant improvement work. This is referred to as *Landlord's Work*. This is done less often because the major retailers prefer to control their own construction. Sometimes a major retailer will negotiate for the landlord to demolish the former improvements, or to install demising walls. In a major remodel, where some tenant spaces are being combined, or a new outside entrance is being cut into an exterior wall, the landlord may do some of the structural work.

Sometimes you can get the landlord to do some generic improvements to the leased premises, but it is more common for the landlord to provide an allowance for the tenant to do its own work.

After the construction work is finished and the store is open, the tenant has to apply to the landlord for the Tenant Allowance money. Typically, there is a section in the lease, usually some added pages, which states how the TA will be paid. In most cases, the TA is paid as a reimbursement after the work is done and paid for by the tenant. The tenant will have to show proof that the contractors have been paid by furnishing lien waivers from each contractor and supplier showing stating that the contractor or supplier has been paid in full.

Note the difference between *"TA"* and *"TI"*. The TI stands for "Tenant Improvements" and refers to the work that the tenant does to improve the space. The TA stands for "Tenant Allowance" and refers to the money that the landlord gives the tenant to build the TI.

HOW MUCH TENANT ALLOWANCE CAN YOU GET?

Not all landlords will give a Tenant Allowance; some will give more. It depends on how badly they want to lease a space to you. If there are a lot of prospective tenants for a good location, the landlord may not have to give any TA at all. If there are several vacancies in a center and they are after new tenants, they may be much more generous with the amount of Tenant Allowance.

The amount of TA also depends on how strong the tenant is. Strong national chain stores with a strong customer draw and proven high-sales stores will be able to negotiate a better deal for Tenant Allowance than a local tenant. Some chain stores can negotiate a Tenant Allowance far in excess of what it costs to actually build the store—the landlord is 'buying' the tenant into the shopping center because of the customer draw that it brings.

In most shopping centers you should be able to negotiate some amount of Tenant Allowance. If you have a decent financial statement, some proven background, and are capable and willing to sign a lease at market rent for a long term, you should get some TA.

The amount of the TA also depends on the value of the lease. The landlord looks at the return (rent) that it will get from the initial investment (TA). If you are going into a shopping center on a short-term deal, a percentage rent deal, or a low rent deal, it is unlikely that you would be able to negotiate some Tenant Allowance. There is no value in those temporary and low-rent leases to pay the landlord back for its investment in your store.

So, it depends. If you can negotiate a low rent or a percentage rent deal for a second-generation space that doesn't need much work, then that might be a better deal for you. But if you are negotiating a permanent, longer-term lease with market rents, then you should try to see if you could get some help with a Tenant Allowance.

A typical deal for a lease in a regional mall in a middle market might be $25 to $35 PSF Tenant Allowance for a lease deal with $20 PSF rent for 10 years, with some rent increases built into the term. Sometimes you can get more—once you understand what you need, you can negotiate and see what you can get.

COSTS OF CONSTRUCTION

The costs to build out a store vary considerably by region and type of shopping center location. To build a new store from a shell, it will cost $60 to $100 per square foot. A small store with a basic build out will likely cost a minimum of $60,000 to $75,000.

Restaurants cost a lot more to build out because of all the plumbing and electrical, and there is a higher cost for the fixtures and restaurant equipment. On the other hand, plain vanilla shell retail spaces in a strip shopping center cost much less to build out.

THE CONSTRUCTION PROCESS

It is no small matter to remodel or build a retail store in a shopping center. Plans have to be drawn by a licensed architect, building permits have to be obtained, a contractor has to be hired, and the construction has to be supervised.

This process is lengthy and complicated if the tenant is building out a complete store, and less complicated if a simple remodel is being done. But whether it is a minor job or a big job, the tenant will have to follow the same steps.

Architectural Plans

The planning process should begin with a store designer or architect who has some experience designing retail stores. Many architects are not interested in doing tenant improvement work, preferring instead to work on longer-standing structures such as buildings. Find an architect with experience in shopping centers. It will pay off.

Most shopping centers have a "Tenant Construction Criteria" handbook. This handbook is mailed to the tenant after the lease is signed, but a copy can probably be obtained from the center management ahead of time to speed up the design process. The plans for the store will have to adhere to the standards for the shopping center. It is a good idea to sit down and review the criteria such as lights, floor coverings, storefront design, etc. with the architect. Many architects who are not experienced in shopping centers just do what they want (or what they are used to), and having to redesign it just costs more money.

The tenant's architectural plans will have to be approved by the landlord's representative. This is usually a person called a *Tenant Coordinator*, perhaps an architect hired by the landlord or the management company to work with tenant improvement construction. Plans are seldom approved as submitted, except for very minor construction. There are almost always going to be revisions or clarifications required. The Tenant Coordinator wants to see everything on the plans. The Tenant Coordinator will work with the tenant's architect until the plans are revised. This process may take a few weeks. Once they are approved, the Tenant Coordinator will stamp a few sets of plans as "approved", and the tenant is ready to apply for a building permit. A licensed general contractor usually obtains the building permit.

If you are taking a second-generation space and doing a small remodel, the same steps will have to be followed. A building permit is required for almost all construction activity in a shopping center, and to get a building permit, you will need some plans approved by the landlord.

General Contractor

After the landlord's tenant coordinator is close to approving the plans, the tenant will want to submit copies to a few general contractors for bids on building the store. The contractors should have some experience in working in shopping centers and doing tenant improvement work.

The contractors will want to know the rules they must follow to build the store. The *Construction Rules* can be obtained from the center management. These rules outline the dos and don'ts the contractors must follow, the security deposit required, fees for shutting off the fire sprinkler system, trash arrangements, and insurance requirements. Some shopping centers require certain subcontractors to work on all projects in the center, such as a roofing contractor to do any roofing work, to make sure the integrity of the roof stays intact. The general contractor will have to use the specified subcontractor for that work, and will need to coordinate with the sub.

After bids are obtained, a contractor is selected by the tenant to build the improvements. Before starting work, the contractor meets with the shopping center management to review the construction plans and scope of work. In some cases, the work may have to be done at night to avoid interfering with neighboring tenants in the shopping center. The contractor will have to provide the center management with proper insurance, a copy of the building permit, the security deposit, a list of subcontractors and suppliers to be used on the job, and a time line for the completion of the construction. If the job is a simple one, the contractor may not use any subcontractors and will do most of the work himself. In a big project, there will likely be many different trades people working on the job.

Construction Process

A barricade wall is usually required in an enclosed mall to wall off the store during the construction process. The contractor usually builds a temporary sheetrock wall. Sometimes, the center will provide the wall and charge the contractor for it. After the wall is up and all pre-construction requirements have been met, the contractor can go to work. In a strip shopping center, with an exterior glass front, a barricade wall is probably not required.

The construction process can take 6 to 12 weeks for a typical tenant build-out. If it is a smaller remodel, it can be done quicker, but it still takes some time. There are a lot of things that need to be completed during this time. The storefront sign will need to be designed, drawn up and submitted for the landlord's approval. The fabrication of the sign takes a few weeks, and should be underway while the store is being built so it can be installed when the store is finished. Equipment and furnishings must be ordered to arrive at the right time so they can be installed in the store when the contractor is ready.

Some centers may provide a temporary staging/storage area for the contractor if one is available. If not, offsite storage will have to be located to store equipment and furnishings before they are installed. Inventory will start arriving before the construction is completed and will have to be stored somewhere until the store is ready for occupancy.

During the construction process, the center management and the tenant coordinator may visit the project site to make sure that building codes and safety codes are being followed and that the project is being built as approved. Experienced contractors who are used to working in shopping centers don't run into many problems, but the occasional inexperienced contractor will run into problems and have many costly re-dos.

If there were any landlord's work to be done, it is usually done before the tenant's contractor takes over the premises. Sometimes, the landlord will use the same contractor, but not always.

Certificate of Occupancy

During the construction process, the contractor will be in touch with the local building department to make sure the work is inspected as it is built. After the final inspection, the building department will issue a *Certificate of Occupancy* stating that the construction was approved and occupancy is allowed. The tenant cannot open for business until the *C of O* is obtained. Sometimes, there are minor problems, such as the placement of a fire extinguisher inside the space, or other small matters, and the building inspector will have to be called back again, extending the completion date.

After the building department has signed off on the construction, and the landlord's tenant coordinator or manager has approved the construction, the tenant is ready to occupy the premises and open the business.

SIGNS

It seems like most small business owners try to save money by investing in a cheap sign. There are almost always disputes between shopping center managers and small tenants who want to hang a substandard signs that doesn't fit with the center's image or criteria.

Almost all shopping centers have a *Sign Criteria*. The sign criteria are usually attached to the lease as an exhibit. There has to be strong control over the size and types of signs that the tenants in a shopping center are allowed to install, or there would be a disarray of all different sizes, shapes and styles of signs.

In an enclosed shopping mall, the landlord would like to see some creativity in signs, with the sign design integral to the design of the storefront. In strip shopping centers, the signs are usually preferred to be of the same size and construction for a more symmetrical look.

You should read the sign criteria carefully, ask questions of the center management, and go through the center to look at other tenants' signs. Then, with some ideas in mind, you should contact some sign companies and start working on a design. Restrictions include the size of the signs allowed, including the overall length of the sign as well as the letter height of the sign. There are often restrictions against certain types of signs, such as exposed neon or painted signs.

If you are going into an enclosed mall, remember that a good sign is integral to the storefront design, as a poor sign looks like it was added on after the fact. A well-designed sign doesn't have to be expensive, but it has to look like it is part of the storefront design. Many small business owners who are taking a second-generation space give little thought to the design of the sign and look for the cheapest alternative that the center will let them get away with. This is a poor approach to creating a successful business. Spend a little extra time looking for a sign maker that can do a creative job with the budget allowed. Go look at some store signs in your center or similar centers and ask for referrals.

STOREFRONTS

In an enclosed mall, the storefront design and appearance are important to encourage the shopper to come into the store. In a strip shopping center, most of the storefronts are the same.

In an enclosed mall, there are different styles of storefronts. Some stores are designed with a wide-open front, and a rolling grille that rolls completely up and out of sight during the day. Some stores have a pop-out storefront with display windows on either side of an open doorway. Some stores inside malls have actual doors that are opened (or propped open), like a Main Street store to give a boutique effect.

If you are using a second-generation store, you should give some thought to the type of business and whether or not it is suited to the existing storefront. Some businesses work well behind a glass display window, and others would die.

The style of the storefront should also work well with the type of store being used. A corner location that was formerly a jewelry store is probably not suitable for other retail uses. The small display windows would work well for jewelry, but not so well with other products.

Similarly, the exterior finish of the storefront should fit in with the products and type of store. A former jewelry store might have a mirrored exterior for a sleek, contemporary look, while a former Western Wear store might have a rough-hewn pine and log exterior. Many times, the exterior finish can be changed without a lot of investment. Some money, time and thought is definitely worth the effort. A store in the wrong type of storefront looks as out of place as a person dressed in the wrong type of clothing.

TENANT IMPROVEMENTS CHECKLIST

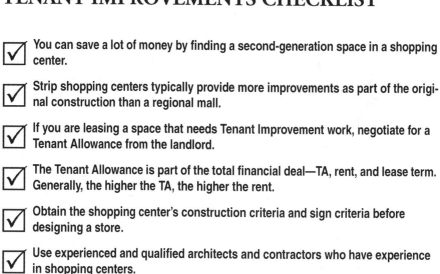

☑ You can save a lot of money by finding a second-generation space in a shopping center.

☑ Strip shopping centers typically provide more improvements as part of the original construction than a regional mall.

☑ If you are leasing a space that needs Tenant Improvement work, negotiate for a Tenant Allowance from the landlord.

☑ The Tenant Allowance is part of the total financial deal—TA, rent, and lease term. Generally, the higher the TA, the higher the rent.

☑ Obtain the shopping center's construction criteria and sign criteria before designing a store.

☑ Use experienced and qualified architects and contractors who have experience in shopping centers.

☑ If you are taking an older space, plan to fix it up as much as possible to make it look appealing and fresh. Invest in a good sign and other elements to make your store look finished and professional.

Index

0-595-28263-6

Made in the USA
San Bernardino, CA
02 June 2015